BIBLICAL
PERSPECTIVES
ON
MONEY

A SCHOLASTIC STUDY
OF GOD'S PRINCIPLES

Compiled by Russell Stevens

VERSION 2

ACKNOWLEDGEMENTS

This workbook, developed as a restatement of God's financial principles for the collegiate arena, involved many hands and minds. Thank you to all who prayed for its completion.

Many co-workers and friends gave input and assisted with editing. I would especially like to thank my extremely patient wife, Kathy. She let me hole up in my office when other things needed to be done, reminding me not to work such long hours that my health, enthusiasm for the task, or my objectivity would be impaired.

My special thanks to Dorene Robertson, who spent a significant amount of time away from her own work to evaluate the budgeting section and suggest improvements.

I am very grateful for Larry Burkett and Howard Dayton, the authors upon whose effort this workbook has been built. Larry Burkett, who went home to be with Our Lord in 2003, was an inspiration and mentor to me. His teaching has been a guiding light for Kathy and me over the past decade, and we miss him greatly. Howard Dayton's teaching and leadership of Crown Financial Ministries are characterized by enthusiasm and vision, encouraging me in my personal walk and work.

Finally, thank you to Chad Cunningham, Sheila Thompson, Liz Hart, and others at the Crown home office for their time and expertise.

Created in Christ's service,

Russ Stevens

© 2007 by Crown Financial Ministries, Inc. (Formerly *Faith and Money: A Non-Traditional Student Workbook*)

ISBN 978-1-56427-177-8

Verses Identified as (NIV) are taken from the *Holy Bible: New International Version*, © 1973, 1978, 1984 by the International Bible Society. Used by permission of Zondervan Bible Publishers.

Verses identified as (TLB) are taken from *The Living Bible*, © 1971 by Tyndale House Publsihers, Wheaton, Illinois. Used by permission.

Verses identified as (NASB) are taken from the *New American Standard Bible®* (Updated Edition), © 1960, 1962, 1963, 1968, 1971, 1972, 1973, 1975, 1977, 1995 by The Lockman Foundation. Used by permission.

April 2007 edition

TABLE OF CONTENTS

PART I. OVERVIEW OF THE WORKBOOK CONTENTS AND HOW TO ACCESS THE PROVIDED RESOURCES

Message to the Non-traditional Student

Much has been written about the appropriate differences between teaching methods for non-traditional students versus those in standard classrooms. Crown's history of designing unique tools for specific groups has enabled them to teach God's financial principles in the most relevant way possible. This manual continues that tradition as it addresses the unique needs of students in a non-traditional setting. We pray that you will apply these principles not only to your class work but also to your personal finances and life.

You will see that the assignments frequently direct you to discuss or debate issues in a group setting. If you are taking this course via e-mail or a web site, those discussions will occur as threaded conversations or possibly in chat rooms. Your instructor will advise you regarding the details.

Galatians 5:1 tells us, *"It is for freedom that Christ has set us free. Stand firm, then, and do not let yourselves be burdened again by a yoke of slavery"* (NIV). Money frequently becomes a new yoke of slavery. Use the principles you learn in this course to regain the freedom that Christ bought for you.

One additional note: Crown has taught hundreds of thousands through Small Group Bible Studies, Financial Seminars, and Budget Coaching. If you have benefited from any of those opportunities, you will have a real advantage in this course. Consider helping other students; the objective is wisdom and faithfulness, not to compete for grades.

Message to the Instructor

The exercises in Part III of this book are available on CD. Answer keys for the exercises in Parts II and III of this book are also on the CD. Part II is in PDF format, and Part III is in Microsoft Excel. These can be used for Web-based classes, e-mail classes, or to supplement on-campus classes. To obtain this CD, please contact Crown Financial Ministries at 770-534-1000 ext. 373 and request the *Biblical Perspectives on Money Instructor's CD*. Verification of status as an instructor at a college, university, or Bible school is required.

This manual is laid out in four sections:

- Part I is the introduction and overview of the contents.

- Part II contains the in-class or on-line principle exercises. Your instructor will choose some or all of these for you to complete in the learning process. While precedent has dictated the order of this manual, your instructor may choose to order subjects differently.

- Part III contains the in-class or online practical application exercises. These will help you learn and apply the budget process.

- Part IV contains a variety of blank forms and additional resources. You may copy the forms to use in class work or for your personal budget.

PART II.   IN-CLASS OR ON-LINE PRINCIPLE EXERCISES

Section 1. *Why Money Matters to God and to Us*

Money really does matter to God. In this section, students will learn from God's Word proper attitudes about the handing of God's resources and who really owns it all.

Key Scripture: Luke 16:11 (modified NASB) *"Therefore if you have not been faithful in the use of worldly wealth, who will entrust the true riches to you?"*

Discussion Exercises:

*NOTE: Remember to read all Scripture passages in context.

- **Exercise 1-1:** Based upon Isaiah 55:8-9, Proverbs 2:10-15, Jeremiah 29:11, Hosea 14:9, Luke 16:11, Matthew 16:26, Philippians 3:8, and other related Scriptures, brainstorm five specific ways in which God's financial principles differ from the world's. For each answer, describe the impact of both God's way and the world's way of handling money on our fellowship with Christ.

- **Exercise 1-2:** Based upon Exodus 19:5, Leviticus 25:23, Deuteronomy 10:14, Psalm 24:1, Psalm 50:10-12, and Haggai 2:8, list at least ten specific things that God owns. Also, tell how His ownership should impact our view of the items listed.

- **Exercise 1-3:** Based upon Genesis 45:4-8, 1 Chronicles 29:11-12, Psalm 34:19-20, Psalm 93:1, Proverbs 21:1, and Romans 8:28, list things that God controls. How should this affect our attitudes and daily activities? Each group member should share a difficult situation he or she has experienced and how the Lord ultimately used it for good in his or her life.

- **Exercise 1-4:** Using the following Scriptures, elaborate on how God distributes material resources and meets our needs: 1 Chronicles 29:14, Psalm 34:9-10, Psalm 65:9, Psalm 127:1-2, Matthew 6:31-33, and Philippians 4:19. Without getting too specific, each group member should give an example of how God distributed a material resource to him or her.

Discussion Question:

1. Looking at Genesis 1:29, Deuteronomy 30:9, Exodus 16:4-35, Numbers 11:31, 1 Kings 17:4-6, 1 Kings 19:5-6, Job 38:41, Psalm 104:14-15, Psalm 145:15, Joel 2:24, Matthew 14:15-21, and Matthew 15:32-38, list specific things God has provided.

Section 2. *Our Part*

The concept of God's ownership of everything leads directly to a realization that stewards have responsibilities in handling those entrusted resources. This section will help students better understand those responsibilities from a Scriptural perspective.

Key Scripture: 1 Chronicles 29:11-12 (TLB) *"Everything in the heavens and earth is yours, O Lord, and this is your kingdom. We adore you as being in control of everything. Riches and honor come from you alone, and you are the Ruler of all mankind; your hand controls power and might, and it is at your discretion that men are made great and given strength."*

Group Debate:

*NOTE: Remember to read all Scripture passages in context.

Read the parable of the talents (Matthew 25:14-30) and debate the two propositions listed below. It is not important that group members agree with the group's proposition, just that they understand it and defend it.

* The process for a debate involves one of the groups putting forth their argument for the assigned proposition followed by the other group doing the same. Next, each group can rebut the other's argument.

- **Debate Proposition 2-1:** A steward is responsible for managing the owner's resources. Based upon that, the steward is justified in taking significant risks in the attempt to earn a good return on the owner's investments.

- **Debate Proposition 2-2:** A steward is responsible to manage the owner's resources. Based upon that, the steward is responsible to avoid risk in the attempt to get some return with no loss of principal.

Discussion Questions:

1. What authority did God give people according to Genesis 1:27-28 and Psalm 8:4-6?

2. What does 1 Corinthians 4:2 require of a steward?

3. Define a steward.

4. Describe God's awareness of our thoughts and actions according to Genesis 6:5, 1 Chronicles 28:9, Psalm 139:1-3, Jeremiah 17:10, and Romans 8:27?

5. What do Matthew 12:36, Romans 14:10-12, 1 Corinthians 4:5, and Hebrews 9:27 tell us of what will happen to each of us in the future? How should this impact the way we live and spend money?

6. Why did the master in Luke 16:1-2 remove the steward from his position? How do you think this principle is applicable today?

7. Describe the principle found in Luke 16:10.

8. According to Luke 16:12, what does Jesus imply about our faithfulness with other people's possessions?

9. According to Matthew 25:24-30, what happens if we are not faithful? Give some specific examples of how these principles apply to you.

Section 3. *Debt*

This section looks at the principles surrounding the subject of debt. Students will learn how God views debt and the responsibility of fulfilling obligations. As stewards, debt can be a significant barrier to faithfulness in following God's will.

Key Scripture: Proverbs 22:7 (TLB) *"Just as the rich rule the poor, so the borrower is servant to the lender."*

Discussion Exercises:
*NOTE: Remember to read all Scripture passages in context.

- **Exercise 3-1:** Determine God's view of debt from the Old Testament. Use Deuteronomy 15:4-6, Deuteronomy 28:12, Deuteronomy 28:43-45, and Proverbs 22:7. Discuss the causes of debt from these and other Scriptures. Determine how the timeless truths in these passages apply to the New Testament believer.

- **Exercise 3-2:** Determine God's view of debt from the New Testament. Use Romans 13:8, 1 Corinthians 7:23, and Galatians 5:1. Determine if debt is prohibited in Scripture. Explain your answer. Consider how debt is encouraged or discouraged in Scripture.

- **Exercise 3-3:** Based upon Psalm 37:21, Proverbs 3:27-28, and Romans 13:7, determine what God says about repayment of debt. Use the story in 2 Kings 4:1-7 to identify principles of getting out of debt. Explain your findings.

- **Exercise 3-4:** Based upon Proverbs 6:1-5, Proverbs 11:15, Proverbs 17:18, and Proverbs 22:26-27, determine what God says about cosigning. Describe the result of a cosigning experience of someone you know.

The *Spending More Money* Cycle

Depression
Want More Things
Not Enough Time
Spend More Money
Surprise Expenses
Overcommitment
No Savings Available
Work More Hours

Section 4. *Counsel*

Another specific subject that affects how a steward manages God's resources is Counsel. This section will allow students to see how important counsel is in the life of a believer and how it affects more areas than just money handling.

Key Scripture: Proverbs 12:15 (NASB) *"The way of a fool is right in his own eyes, but a wise man is he who listens to counsel."*

Discussion Exercises:
*NOTE: Remember to read all Scripture passages in context.

- **Exercise 4-1:** List some scriptural benefits of seeking counsel. Use Psalm 1:1-3, Proverbs 11:14, Proverbs 12:15, Proverbs 13:10, Proverbs 15:22, Proverbs 19:20, Proverbs 27:9-10, and Ecclesiastes 4:13. Create a list of what stops you from seeking counsel.

- **Exercise 4-2:** From personal experience as well as the Scriptures, discuss the ways God counsels His people and the consequences of not seeking His counsel. Use Joshua 9:14-20, Judges 20:27-28, Psalm 16:7, Psalm 25:12, Psalm 32:8, Psalm 106:13-15, Isaiah 48:17-19, and John 16:13.

- **Exercise 4-3:** List some reasons why we should seek God's counsel through Scripture and the benefits of doing so. Use Psalm 1:2-3, Psalm 19:8, Psalm 119:24, Psalm 119:105, Psalm 119:98-100, Matthew 7:24, 2 Timothy 3:16-17, and Hebrews 4:12.

- **Exercise 4-4:** From Genesis 2:24, Exodus 23:2, Psalm 1:1-3, Proverbs 1:8-9, Proverbs 11:14, Proverbs 12:5, Ecclesiastes 4:9-12, and 1 Corinthians 5:11, compile lists of who should and who should not be our counselors.

Section 5. *Honesty*

God expects His children to follow the example of Christ in exhibiting total honesty in all their dealings. The Scriptures discussed in this section will give students a better understanding of the benefits of being honest and the pitfalls of being dishonest.

Key Scripture: Leviticus 9:11 (NASB) *"You shall not steal, nor deal falsely, nor lie to one another."*

Discussion Exercises:
*NOTE: Remember to read all Scripture passages in context.

- **Exercise 5-1:** Based upon Leviticus 19:11-13, Deuteronomy 25:13-16, Joshua 7, Psalm 101:7, Proverbs 11:11, Proverbs 19:1, Proverbs 20:7, Ephesians 4:25, and 1 Peter 3:10, discuss

    - God's requirements for His children to act honestly.

    - and what motivates us to act dishonestly.

- **Exercise 5-2:** Using Deuteronomy 27:17-19, Proverbs 11:3, Proverbs 28:3, Proverbs 28:16, Proverbs 29:12, and 1 Timothy 3:8, examine the consequences of dishonesty in leaders.

- **Exercise 5-3:** List some benefits of honesty. Use Deuteronomy 25:15, Psalm 15:1-5, Proverbs 2:7, Proverbs 10:9, Proverbs 28:13, Isaiah 33:15-16, and Romans 13:9-10.

- **Exercise 5-4:** Determine how dishonesty affects relationships with God and with others. Discuss the relevance of restitution. Use Exodus 22:1-4, Numbers 5:5-8, Psalm 101:7, Proverbs 6:30-31, Proverbs 13:11, Proverbs 15:4, Proverbs 26:28, Micah 6:12-13, and Luke 19:8.

Discussion Questions:
1. What do Exodus 23:8, Proverbs 15:27, Proverbs 17:23, Proverbs 29:4, and 1 Timothy 6:10 tell of God's position on bribes?
2. Describe any personal experience with bribes, either offered, taken, or given.

Section 6. *Giving*

A major part of stewardship is giving. This section uses God's word to explain how God views giving and how a faithful steward can experience freedom through generosity.

Key Scripture: Acts 20:35 (NASB) *"Remember the words of the Lord Jesus that He Himself said, 'It is more blessed to give than to receive.'"*

Discussion Exercises:
*NOTE: Remember to read all Scripture passages in context.

- **Exercise 6-1:** Identify and discuss the benefits of giving and God's attitude about His children giving to others. Also discuss how you think God expects believers to differ from the rest of the world in giving. Use Deuteronomy 15:7, Proverbs 11:24-25, Matthew 6:20, Matthew 19:21, Luke 6:38, Acts 4:34-35, Acts 20:35, Romans 12:8, and 1 Timothy 6:18-19.

- **Exercise 6-2:** Examine the following Scriptures about tithing and develop a history of tithing and a summary of the benefits. Use Genesis 14:20, Genesis 28:22, Leviticus 27:30, 2 Chronicles 31:5, Malachi 3:8-10, Matthew 23:23, Luke 12:34, and Hebrews 7:1-9.

- **Exercise 6-3:** Based upon Proverbs 25:21, Proverbs 31:20, Isaiah 58:6-11, Luke 12:33, Acts 20:35, Galatians 6:6, 1 Timothy 5:17-18, and James 1:27, who are proper recipients of our giving.

- **Exercise 6-4:** Based upon Deuteronomy 15:7, Proverbs 19:17, Proverbs 22:9, Matthew 10:42, Matthew 19:21, and Galatians 2:9-10, discuss the benefits of giving to the poor, and how Jesus identifies with them.

Discussion Question:
1. What do Matthew 15:4-6 and 1 Timothy 5:8 say about caring for our families?

Section 7. *Work*

Work is a legitimate means through which God's provision can flow. This section will help the students to gain a proper view of work in God's plan for the faithful steward.

Key Scripture: Colossians 23:24 (NASB) *"Whatever you do, do your work heartily, as for the Lord rather than for men. . . . It is the Lord Christ whom you serve."*

Discussion Exercises:

*NOTE: Remember to read all Scripture passages in context.

- **Exercise 7-1:** Using the following Scriptures, determine whether God ordained work before the Fall or only after it. Also, list biblical principles regarding how we are to work. Use Genesis 2:15, Genesis 3:17-19, Genesis 39:2-5, Exodus 20:9, Exodus 36:1-2, and 2 Thessalonians 3:10-12.

- **Exercise 7-2:** List the employer and employee responsibilities in 1 Corinthians 4:2, Ephesians 6:5-9, Colossians 3:22-25, James 4:17, and 1 Peter 2:18.

- **Exercise 7-3:** Using the following Scriptures, develop a list of appropriate work habits: Exodus 23:12, Exodus 34:21, 1 Chronicles 22:15-16, Proverbs 6:6-11, Proverbs 18:9, Proverbs 24:27, 2 Thessalonians 3:7-9, and Titus 2:9.

- **Exercise 7-4:** Using Colossians 3:23-24, determine for whom we really work. Based upon Psalm 1:1, Proverbs 24:1, and 2 Corinthians 6:14-18, list some benefits and cautions for partnerships. Using Numbers 8:24-26 and Proverbs 24:33-34 as a backdrop, how would you view the subject of retirement.

Priorities

Spouse

Work   **God**   Children

Ministry

Section 8. *Investing*

Investing, like work, is another of God's chosen areas of provision. In this section, students will learn God's principles of investing and to implement investing as a tool to multiply resources.

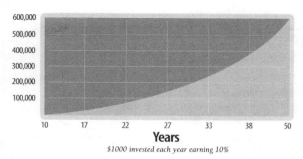
Years
$1000 invested each year earning 10%

Key Scripture: Proverbs 21:5 (TLB) *"Steady plodding brings prosperity; hasty speculation brings poverty."*

Group Debate:

*NOTE: Remember to read all Scripture passages in context.

Debate the two propositions listed below. It is not important that group members agree with the group's proposition, just that they understand it and defend it.

- **Debate Proposition 8-1:** We are to trust God to care for us; therefore, saving is hoarding money that should be used for God's current work. Use Job 31:24-28, Psalm 23, Proverbs 3:5-6, Ecclesiastes 11:1, Matthew 6:19, Matthew 6:25-34, Philippians 4:19, and 1 Timothy 6:17.

- **Debate Proposition 8-2:** We should save everything that is not absolutely necessary to give or spend. God wants us to care for ourselves with His resources. Use Genesis 41:34-36, Proverbs 6:6-8, Proverbs 21:20, Proverbs 22:3, Proverbs 27:1, Proverbs 30:24-25, and John 6:12.

Discussion Exercises:

- **Exercise 8-1:** Provide at least two answers to each of the following questions. What does 1 Timothy 5:8 suggest as valid reasons to save? What does 1 Timothy 6:9-10 suggest as invalid reasons to save?

- **Exercise 8-2:** Develop investment principles suggested by the following Scriptures.

Proverbs 12:5	Proverbs 13:4
Proverbs 21:5	Proverbs 24:27
Proverbs 27:23-24	Proverbs 28:20
Ecclesiastes 3:1	Ecclesiastes 11:2
Luke 12:33	

- **Exercise 8-3:** Develop inheritance principles suggested by the following Scriptures.

Genesis 24:35-36	Numbers 27:8-11
Psalm 39:6	Proverbs 20:21
Proverbs 22:6	Matthew 6:19
2 Corinthians 12:14	1 Timothy 6:7

- **Exercise 8-4:** Using the Scriptures below, discuss the responsibility for and practical methods of training our children to handle money. Also discuss ideas of how to teach children to save, invest, be cheerful givers, and avoid the bondage of debt. Use Deuteronomy 4:9, Deuteronomy 11:18-19, Psalm 19:7-8, Psalm 78:5-6, Proverbs 22:6, Ephesians 6:4 and 2 Timothy 1:5.

Section 9. *Perspective*

This section will teach an overview of money related subjects to put money handling into perspective. Students will learn usable principles from the lives of famous biblical characters. They will also learn the principles of contentment, lifestyle, paying taxes, the danger of money, and why wicked people prosper.

Key Scripture: Philippians 4:11-13 (NASB) *"I have learned to be content in whatever circumstances I am. I know how to get along with humble means, and I also know how to live in prosperity. . . . I can do all things through Him who strengthens me."*

Group Debate:
*NOTE: Remember to read all Scripture passages in context.

Debate the two propositions listed below. It is not important that group members agree with the group's proposition, just that they understand it and defend it.

- **Debate Proposition 9-1:** Riches are dangerous and should be avoided. Poverty is a form of godliness. Use Genesis 13:5-11; Matthew 13:7, 22; Matthew 19:16-23; 2 Corinthians 8:9; Philippians 3:8; and other applicable verses.

- **Debate Proposition 9-2:** Riches are God's blessing and should be sought and used to do good works with them. Use Deuteronomy 7:12-14, Deuteronomy 30:15-16, Psalm 1:1-3, Hebrews 13:16, 1 Timothy 6:18-19, 1 Peter 2:12, and other applicable verses.

Discussion Exercises:
For Exercises 9-1 through 9-4: Reflect on the life of the assigned biblical character. Answer the questions: Did these men experience both poverty and riches? Was the poverty either from sin or from lack of faith? Should all Christians be prosperous?

- **Exercise 9-1:** Job (Book of Job)

- **Exercise 9-2:** Joseph (Genesis chapters 37, 39, and 50)

- **Exercise 9-3:** David (1 Samuel and 1 Kings 2)

- **Exercise 9-4:** Paul (the Book of Acts and the Pauline letters).

- **Exercise 9-5:** Wicked people do prosper. Based upon Psalm 73:1-20, Ecclesiastes 2:26, Jeremiah 12:1-2, James 5:3, and Revelation 3:17, discuss prosperity and testing of the wicked.

- **Exercise 9-6:** Discuss what the following Scriptures say about contentment: Proverbs 15:16, Luke 3:14, Philippians 4:11-13, 1 Timothy 6:6-8, and Hebrews 13:5.

- **Exercise 9-7:** Discuss what the following Scriptures say about paying our taxes: Matthew 22:17-21, Romans 13:1-7, and Titus 3:1. Also discuss what James 2:1-9 says about showing favoritism.

- **Exercise 9-8:** Define the lifestyle that God intends for Christians from the following Scriptures: Matthew 6:25, Mark 8:36-37, Acts 4:32-37, Philippians 4:19, 1 Thessalonians 4:11-12, and James 4:4.

Section 10. *Eternity*

Life on earth is short and eternity is forever. This section will teach students how a proper view of eternity affects a steward's purpose and clarifies focus in relation to financial matters.

Key Scripture: Mark 8:36 (NASB) *"What does it profit a man to gain the whole world, and forfeit his soul?"*

Discussion Exercises:
*NOTE: Remember to read all Scripture passages in context.

- **Exercise 10-1:** How long is life on earth? Use the following Scriptures for your answer: Psalm 39:4-6, Psalm 90:10, Psalm 103:13-16, and James 4:14.

- **Exercise 10-2:** Describe the Christian's identity here on earth using the following Scriptures: 1 Chronicles 29:15 and Philippians 3:20. Based upon Psalm 102:25-26, Isaiah 34:4, and 2 Peter 3:10-13, describe the fate of the earth and its impact on how we should live.

- **Exercise 10-3:** According to Ecclesiastes 12:13-14, Matthew 16:27, 1 Corinthians 4:5, Hebrews 9:27, and Revelation 20:12, describe the future of every person.

- **Exercise 10-4:** Based upon 1 Corinthians 3:11-15 and 1 Peter 1:6-7, describe works that will be burned and works that will be rewarded at the end of life. List what our priorities should be according to Matthew 5:3-11, John 6:27, and 2 Corinthians 4:18.

PART III   IN-CLASS OR ON-LINE PRACTICAL APPLICATIONS

The exercises in this section may be completed via three different media. Your instructor will notify you of the appropriate medium for your class.

- One medium is the hard-copy lists and forms printed in each section of this workbook. Each practical application section starts with a description of the assignment followed by a copy of the blank form and the data to be used in completing the form. Your instructor will indicate how you are to submit completed assignments.

- A second medium is e-mail. The e-mail forms are provided in a spreadsheet format with multiple worksheets within one Excel workbook for each section. The data and forms are identical between the paper version and the spreadsheet version. Each worksheet contains either blank forms to be completed or pages of data that are necessary to complete the assignment.

  Note: If you aren't sure how to use Excel or how to use multiple worksheets within an Excel workbook, select "Help" from the Excel menu and then select "Show the Office Assistant." Click on the icon that pops up on your screen, type "Worksheet" in the search box, and click on Search. By selecting different topics listed, you should be able to learn enough to do the exercises. In addition, there are excellent tutorials on the Internet. Try a Web search on "Microsoft Excel Tutorials."

  Complete each assignment by entering data into the appropriate cells in the blank form in the workbook and "saving" it. The instructor will advise whether to submit assignments electronically or print and turn them in.

- A third medium is to access the forms on a Web-based learning system. These are also in Excel workbooks as described previously. Your instructor will indicate the proper way to submit the completed assignments.

Please note:
1. Although the assignments are designed to approximate real budget situations, each assignment stands by itself and the numbers do not carry from one assignment to the next. You are encouraged to use the blank forms provided in the appendix to create and run your own budget. By the time you finish this class, you will have learned the hows and whys of doing your own budget.

2. Sample numbers from the assignments may not seem applicable to your personal situation. The numbers provided are based loosely upon national database averages. They will seem high in some areas of the country and low in others.

The situations used in the assignments are also relative to different household types (family, single, single parent). Part III, Section 6.2 contains Budget Guideline tables for differing household configurations and differing housing-cost areas. When creating your own budget, please use the table that most closely approximates your individual situation.

Section 1. *Monthly Estimated Budget (Form 1)*

Forms and schedules included:
1. Monthly Estimated Budget form (blank)
2. List of Monthly Income and Payroll Deductions
3. List of Checks Written
4. Cash Spending list
5. Credit Card Spending list

Introduction:

A family of four has wisely prepared to create their first budget. They gathered all recent financial transactions, including every cash expenditure, and then organized them by spending method. The resulting lists they created are schedules 2 through 5. These lists are then used to fill out the Monthly Estimated Budget form.

Purpose of Form:

The Monthly Estimated Budget form is a place to summarize a household's average monthly spending. Many families do not have a clear picture of their income and expenses; they may just be vaguely aware that credit card debt is increasing. Completing this form can be painful as reality is brought into focus. Ignoring reality and continuing with out-of-control financial habits, however, is ultimately much more painful.

Anyone who attempts to create a budget—or even fill out the Monthly Estimated Budget Form—without first tracking all spending for a month will experience discouraging confusion as they guess at numbers. It's important to understand that completing schedules 2-5 should be the first step. It will help clarify the process and guard against overlooking less obvious expenses.

Keep in mind that some spending is irregular or non-monthly. Although irregular expenses may not be part of the class assignment, they are usually part of a real household budget. These include expenses such as annual life insurance payments, semi-annual car insurance payments, periodic teeth cleaning, Christmas and other gifts, and annual vacations. To ensure that these important spending items are accounted for, an annual estimate must be determined and then divided by 12. This figure is then inserted into the Monthly Estimated Budget form.

This form and its prerequisite schedules 2-5 comprise the first major step in the budget process. It usually does not balance at first. Don't let this deter you. Further learning steps will help you make decisions about necessary adjustments.

Assignment:

Please Note: All forms in this section include numbers to use for correct completion of the assignments. DO NOT USE your own personal budget numbers. Use the sample numbers provided.

Compile and enter all of the data from schedules 2 though 5 (using provided numbers) into the correct categories and lines of the blank Monthly Estimated Budget form (schedule 1). Since accuracy is important, calculate the bottom line by totaling the income and the spending using the schedules. The difference between the two totals will be the target for Surplus or Deficit on the Monthly Estimated Budget form.

To help identify the correct categories for various expenses, most of the categories on the Monthly Estimated Budget form include itemized lists. For a more detailed description of what each category should contain, see Part III, Section 6.1 (Additional Schedules— Understanding the Monthly Income and Spending Categories).

Submission of Completed Assignment:
Follow instructions provided by the instructor.

1. Monthly Estimated Budget

NAME OF STUDENT _____

AS OF JANUARY 2005

Monthly Income

GROSS INCOME PER MONTH:

Salary	_____
Interest	_____
Dividends	_____
Other	_____
Total Gross Income Per Month	[ ]

LESS:

1. **Tithe/Giving** [   ]

2. **Tax (Fed, State, FICA)** [   ]

   NET SPENDABLE INCOME [   ]

Monthly Living Expenses

3. **Housing**

Mortgage (Rent)	_____
Insurance	_____
Taxes	_____
Electricity	_____
Gas	_____
Water	_____
Sanitation	_____
Telephone	_____
Maintenance	_____
Assoc. Dues	_____
Other	_____
Total Housing	[ ]

4. **Food** [   ]

5. **Automobile**

Payments	_____
Gas/Oil	_____
Insurance	_____
License/Taxes	_____
Maint/Repair	_____
Replace	_____
Total Automobile	[ ]

6. **Insurance**

Life	_____
Medical	_____
Other	_____
Total Insurance	[ ]

7. **Debts**

Credit Cards	_____
Loans/Notes	_____
Other	_____
Total Debts	[ ]

8. **Entertainment & Recreation**

Eating Out	_____
Baby Sitters	_____
Activities/Trips	_____
Vacation	_____
Other	_____
Total Entertainment & Recreation	[ ]

9. **Clothing** [   ]

10. **Savings** [   ]

11. **Medical Expenses**

Doctor	_____
Dentist	_____
Prescriptions	_____
Other	_____
Total Medical Expenses	[ ]

12. **Miscellaneous**

Cosmetics	_____
Beauty/Barber	_____
Laundry/Cleaning	_____
Allowances	_____
Pets	_____
Subscriptions	_____
Gifts	_____
Christmas Gifts	_____
Other	_____
Total Miscellaneous	[ ]

13. **Investments** [   ]

14. **School/Child Care**

Tuition	_____
Materials	_____
Transportation	_____
Day Care	_____
Total School/Child Care	[ ]

   TOTAL LIVING EXPENSES [   ]

Income Versus Living Expenses

Net Spendable Income	[ ]
Less	
Total Living Expenses	[ ]
Surplus or Deficit	[ ]

19

2. List of Monthly Income and Payroll Deductions for January, 2005

* Gleaned from pay stubs and bank statements

			Total
Interest Earned on Savings			$2.50

Monthly Pay	Husband	Wife	Total
Gross Pay	$3,500.00	$1,500.00	$5,000.00
Payroll Deductions			
Federal Income Tax	(585.40)	(136.60)	(722.00)
FICA	(207.90)	(89.10)	(297.00)
Medicare	(48.65)	(20.85)	(69.50)
State Income Tax	(225.62)	(15.98)	(241.60)
State Disability Tax	(30.10)	(12.90)	(43.00)
Income after Taxes	2,402.33	1,224.57	3,626.90
Other Deductions			
Medical Insurance	(52.35)	(12.50)	(64.85)
401k Deduction			
(Retirement Investment)	(105.00)	(45.00)	(150.00)
Net Paycheck	$2,244.98	$1,167.07	$3,412.05

3. List of Checks Written for January 2005

Check #	Description	Check Amount
876	AllCoast Financial - Mortgage	975.35
877	The Gas Company	58.00
878	Ralph's Market	149.56
879	Car Payment	235.25
880	Community Church	20.00
881	Whole Foods Market	15.00
882	National Student Loan Corporation	85.00
883	City Water Department	85.50
EFT	Bank @ Home monthly fee	3.95
884	Consolidated Electric	99.75
885	Cityview Mastercard	25.00
886	Community Church	20.00
887	The Hair Affair	27.50
888	County Tax Assessor (monthly taxes)	40.00
889	Community Church	20.00
890	Creditcorp Platinum Plus Visa	31.00
891	State Phone Company	28.00
892	Car Payment	147.35
893	Equity Life Insurance	45.00
894	Auto Insurance	155.35
895	Community Church	20.00
896	Auto Insurance	105.15
897	House Insurance	130.15
898	Homeowners Association Monthly Fee	85.00

Note: EFT (above) stands for Electronic Funds Transfer and is usually a charge that the bank assesses on a regular basis without the use of a check.

4. Cash Spending for January 2005

* From Receipts and Pocket Notebook

Description	Amount
Gourmet Coffee / Tea	2.70
Fast Food	15.35
Contribute to Boss's Birthday Gift	10.00
Fast Food	15.87
Car Wash	6.99
Hallmark Cards (gifts)	12.45
Cat Food	18.54
Allowances to Kids	25.00
Gourmet Coffee / Tea	2.95
Fast Food	12.25
County Fair Parking	7.50
County Fair Tickets	48.00
Food at Fair	74.56
Fast Food	19.57
Gourmet Coffee / Tea	4.15
Fast Food	15.45
Restaurant	20.68
Allowances to Kids	25.00

5.   Credit Card Spending for January 2005
* Listed from Credit Card Receipts and Statements

Spent for:	Amount
Prescription	10.00
Groceries	39.45
Monthly Credit Protection Fee	25.00
Gift Card	25.00
Medical Testing	13.30
Prescription	5.00
Gas in Car	6.90
Restaurant	21.32
Long Distance Service	6.36
Gas in Car	15.86
Stamps	12.50
Groceries	19.53
Gifts	30.70
Home Repair	11.32
Shoes	35.55
Groceries	23.86
Gas in Car	13.63
Groceries	32.56
Restaurant	64.64
Home Repair	69.25
Restaurant	19.66
Auto Repair	116.85
Restaurant	35.89
Gas in Car	29.19
Haircut	20.00
Doctor	25.00
Prescription	15.00
Clothing	12.93
Restaurant	10.85

Section 2. *List of Debts*

Forms and schedules included:

1. List of Debts form (blank)
2. Sears payment coupon
3. National School Loan payment coupon
4. MasterCard payment coupon
5. Nordstroms payment coupon
6. Payment coupon for house mortgage
7. Mervyns payment coupon
8. Payment coupon for Toyota van
9. Visa payment coupon

Introduction:

A single parent of two has kept copies of the last month's payment coupons, which included all the data needed to fill out this form. The copies of the coupons are in schedules 2 through 9. Completing a list of debts is a critical step in determining the starting point for paying them down and paying them off. In completing this form, she has correctly noted just the minimum payment amounts, not the amounts that she may have been paying.

Purpose of Form:

The List of Debts form enables a household to see exactly what their debt situation is. A high percentage of people have only a vague idea, avoiding the knowledge that would help them take appropriate action until they have lost all borrowing power. By that time their accumulated debt is a monster. Knowing the truth is the beginning of freedom; avoiding it deepens and prolongs bondage.

The process of bringing a budget into balance can be derailed after months of hard work when a bill, which was initially missed, arrives without warning. An extra payment squeezed into an already tight budget could destroy the possibility of making the budget balance, or worse yet, discourage the family from proceeding further in the budgeting process. Complete the list with care, making sure that you don't overlook any debts including those with irregular or balloon payments.

Assignment:

Please Note: All forms in this section include numbers to use for correct completion of the assignments. DO NOT USE your own personal budget numbers. Use the sample numbers provideds.

Enter all of the data from schedules 2 though 9 onto the List of Debts form (schedule 1). Calculate the bottom lines by totaling all the minimum payments due and all the total balances due using the provided schedules. Since the List of Debts needs to be totaled as part of the assignment, the bottom line for both amounts will give a target to ensure that the task has been done accurately.

The correct way to complete this form is to list the debts from highest balance due to lowest balance due in the order of total balance due (payoff). When entering the payment due amount, use the minimum amount due for each debt rather than any extra payment that might be made. Doing this will help to pay down or pay off the debts in a faster, more logical manner. This process is explained in Part IV, Section 2—the Debt Paydown section of this workbook.

To calculate the number of payments left for revolving accounts (credit cards, lines of credit, and so on), you may need to use some online tools or financial formulas. There are resources for that process listed in Part IV Section 3—Online Tools. For mortgages, car loans, or the like, payoff amounts may be obtained by calling the lender. For this assignment, they are provided.

Total the two columns containing the payoff amounts and the monthly payment amounts to set a starting point for the budget process.

Submission of Completed Assignment:
Follow instructions provided by the instructor.

1. List of Debts

NAME OF STUDENT _____

AS OF JANUARY 1, 2005

Creditor/Item Purchased	Monthly Payment	Balance Due	Payment Date (Day of Mo.)	Scheduled Payoff Date	Interest Rate	Past Due Amount
Total						

2. Sears Payment Coupon

Sears Payment Center
PO Box 182149
Columbus, OH 43218-2149

Janet Jones
11 Division Street
Anytown, Anystate 11113

Credit Card Payment Coupon

Account Number   Jones22459

Prior Balance: $147.00

Last Payment   10.00
        Interest   3.00
        Principal   7.00

Next Payment of $10.00
due on   January 25, 2005
Make check payable to Sears

Current Balance $140.00

Interest applied on average outstanding balance at the rate of .24 (24%) per annum

3. National School Loan Coupon

Payment Due: $200.00
Payment Due On: January 3, 2005

Student Name:

Amount Being Paid:

Jones, Janet J.
11 Division Street
Anytown, Anystate 11113

Last Payment made: December 2, 2004
Loan Principal Outstanding: $7,794.00

National School Loan Administration
PO Box 12345

Interest Rate: 14.50%   Washington, DC 20001
Payments Left: 53

*Please write your account number on your check and be sure
the mailing address shows through the envelope window.*

4. Nbank MasterCard Coupon

Nbank Credit Corporation
23 East Pikes Peak Avenue
Colorado Springs, CO 80903

Janet Jones
11 Division Street
Anytown, Anystate 11113

Credit Card Payment Coupon

Account Number   14598Jones7845300

Prior Balance: $5,418.16

Last Payment   122.00
         Interest   84.84
         Principal   37.16

Next Payment of $118.00
due on   January 17, 2005
Make check payable to NBank

Current Balance $5,381.00

Interest applied on average outstanding balance at the rate of .24 (24%) per annum

5. Nordstrom Coupon

Nordstrom Company
1617 Sixth Avenue
Seattle, WA 98101

Janet Jones
11 Division Street
Anytown, Anystate 11113

Credit Card Payment Coupon

Account Number   5467-234-08887

Prior Balance: $1,294.74

Last Payment   28.00
         Interest   22.66
         Principal   5.34

Next Payment of $27.00
due on   January 25, 2005
Make check payable to Nordstrom

Current Balance $1,289.00

Interest applied on average outstanding balance at the rate of .21 (21%) per annum

6. Mortgage Coupon

Payment Due: $1,530.00
Payment Due On: January 10, 2005

Jones, Janet J.   Amount Being Paid:
11 Division Street   Extra Principal Paid:
Anytown, Anystate 11113

Last Payment made: December 9, 2004
Loan Principal Outstanding: $191,560.35

                                First Mortgage and Loan Company
Interest Rate: 8.75%   12 Civic Center Plaza
Payments Left: 336   Santa Ana, CA 92705

Please write your account number on your check and be sure
the mailing address shows through the envelope window.

7. Mervyn's Coupon

Mervyn's Credit Assurance   Janet Jones
22301 Foothill Blvd   11 Division Street
Hayward, CA 94541   Anytown, Anystate 11113

Credit Card Payment Coupon   Account Number   9264898-45826-11546

Prior Balance: $452.85

Last Payment   11.00
        Interest   7.60   Next Payment of $10.00
        Principal 3.40   due on   January 1, 2005
                                  Make check payable to Mervyn's
Current Balance $449.45

Interest applied on average outstanding balance at the rate of .198 (19.8%) per annum

8. Auto Finance Corp Coupon

Payment Due: $321.00

Payment Due On: January 15, 2005

Jones, Janet J.
11 Division Street
Anytown, Anystate 11113

Amount Being Paid:

Last Payment made: December 9, 2004
Loan Principal Outstanding: $11,668.85

Auto Finance Corp
23554 Beach Blvd, Suite E
Huntington Beach, CA 92647

Interest Rate: 11.50%

Payments Left: 45

*Please write your account number on your check and be sure
the mailing address shows through the envelope window.*

9. Super Bank Coupon

Super Bank Cardholder Services
23 Longhorn Lane
Dallas, TX 75243

Janet Jones
11 Division Street
Anytown, Anystate 11113

Credit Card Payment Coupon

Account Number   3720-15668-58965

Prior Balance: $4,975.48

Last Payment   110.00
        Interest   83.47
        Principal   26.53

Next Payment of $109.00
due on   January 1, 2005
Make check payable to Super Bank

Current Balance $4,948.95

Interest applied on average outstanding balance at the rate of .198 (19.8%) per annum

Section 3. Budget Analysis

Forms and schedules included:

1. Budget Analysis form (blank)
2. Monthly Estimated Budget form

Introduction:

A single adult has calculated the average of what he has been spending each month on the Monthly Estimated Budget form. He is out of balance, spending more than he earns.

Purpose of Form:

The Budget Analysis form summarizes current spending, compares it to a guideline, and indicates where up or down spending adjustments may be necessary to bring the total budget into balance. When doing a personal budget, bathe the process in prayer. How we handle our money has an eternal impact, making budgeting a spiritual process.

One thing to keep in mind while completing this form is that it is usually necessary to have money allocated in all categories (except possibly School/Child Care and Investments). This is particularly true of the Savings and Clothing categories. Quite often in a tight budget situation, these two categories are neglected. Reality, however, shows that clothing is usually bought using credit cards, which increases debt. Savings is necessary to start and complete the process of getting out of debt. Without savings, the inevitable emergencies of daily living are also put on credit cards, which is a step backwards in a debt reduction plan.

The one category that can be ignored if it is not being used is School/Child Care. If there is no spending or planned spending in that category, no budget is needed. In the near term, the Investment category also can be zero. However, the future for those who do not have income to supplement their Social Security may be difficult. Investments in the form of long-term savings will be necessary for retirement or other future goals.

Note: Selection of the column to use in most of the schedules is based upon gross annual income. When using Percentage Guideline schedules other than the Single Adult, and when the gross annual income falls between the columns, use the column with the lower gross annual income. Also, take note of the "extra" categories listed on most of the Guideline Percentage schedules. If those categories are being used, spending in other categories will need to be reduced to bring the budget into balance.

Assignment:

Please Note: All forms in this section include numbers to use for correct completion of the assignments. DO NOT USE your own personal budget numbers. Use the sample numbers provided.

Step One: Fill in the Income per Month and the Income per Year at the top of the Budget Analysis form. The Income per Year should be the Income per Month multiplied by 12.

31

Step Two: Using the data from the provided Monthly Estimated Budget form (schedule 2), fill in the Existing Budget column of the Budget Analysis worksheet. Be sure that totaling and subtracting the Discretionary Spending number in this column from the Net Spendable Income in this column results in the same bottom line as is on the Monthly Estimated Budget.

Step Three: From workbook Part III, Section 6.2—Percentage Guideline Schedules, use the guideline percentages for a Single Adult to calculate the correct numbers for the Guideline Budget column. To complete this column, follow the steps below.

1. Determine which column on the Percentage Guideline Schedule is appropriate. On the Single Adult schedule, column selection is based upon income and living arrangements. For the purpose of this exercise, use the Living Alone with $32,000 Gross Income column percentages. Circle this column for reference during this assignment.

2. Multiply the Income per Month from the top of the Budget Analysis form by the percentage for the Tithe category in the circled column in the Percentage Guideline Schedule and place the result in the top box of the Guideline Budget column. Do the same for the Tax percentage using the Tax category amount and place the result in the second box. Remember that the Income per Month is not necessarily the same as the Guideline Monthly Gross Income. While doing these two calculations, be sure to use the Income per Month from the Budget Analysis form.

3. Subtract the amounts in the first two boxes in the Guideline Budget column from the Income per Month and enter the result in the Net Spendable Income box.

4. Using the Net Spendable Income amount (not the Income per Month amount) and the percentages from the circled column in the Percentage Guideline schedule, calculate the contents of the remaining boxes in the Guideline Budget column.

5. Total the amounts in the Guideline Budget column, categories 3 through 14, and place the result in the Total Living Expenses box. This number will probably not be the same as the Net Spendable Income. In this exercise, the number in the Total Living Expenses box will exceed the Net Spendable Income by about 10 percent of the gross income. This is because there will be a number in the School/Child Care box (which is an extra category).

Step Four: Line by line, subtract the amounts in the Existing Budget column from the amounts in the Guideline Budget column and enter the results in boxes in the Difference column.

Step Five: The New Monthly Budget column is where the new monthly budget will be created. To create this new budget, examine the line in the Difference column where the difference is the biggest, positive or negative.

1. A negative number indicates more spending than the guideline would suggest. Analyze the components of the category from the Monthly Income and Expense form to find places where spending might be reduced. This action needs to be realistic. It is not realistic to arbitrarily cut a $2,000 Housing category by $800 when rent alone is $1,250. Keep notes of every change you make and the justifications behind

the changes. Enter the new number into the appropriate line of the New Monthly Budget column.

2. A positive number indicates that spending in the category may need to increase. Decide if this is a category that needs a higher allocation (most often true in Savings) and enter the new number into the appropriate line of the New Monthly Budget column.

3. Continue with the same steps for the remainder of the New Monthly Budget column. Recognize that every such decision in real life is a spiritual decision.

4. After you have completed the previous three steps and made appropriate adjustments, calculate the new Net Spendable Income and Total Living Expenses for the New Monthly Budget. If the Net Spendable Income does not equal Total Living Expenses, go back and redo these steps until the New Monthly Budget column is in balance.

Step Six: Submit the completed form with a balanced budget in the New Monthly Budget column. Important: Along with the balanced budget, submit an itemized listing of each change made and the rationale behind each change.

Submission of Completed Assignment:

Follow instructions provided by the instructor.

1.   Budget Analysis

NAME OF STUDENT _____

Income per Year: _____
Income per Month   _____

Monthly Payment Category	Existing Budget	Guideline Budget	Difference + or –	New Monthly Budget
1. Tithe/Giving				
2. Tax				
Net Spendable Income				
3. Housing				
4. Food				
5. Automobile				
6. Insurance				
7. Debts				
8. Entertain & Recreation				
9. Clothing				
10. Savings				
11. Medical				
12. Miscellaneous				
13. Investments				
14. School/Child Care				
Total Living Expenses (Total of 3-14)				
Difference				

2.   Monthly Estimated Budget

MALE SINGLE ADULT
AS OF JANUARY 2005

Monthly Income

GROSS INCOME PER MONTH:

Salary	2,200	
Interest	50	
Dividends		
Other		
Total Gross Income Per Month		2,250

LESS:

1.	Tithe/Giving		160
2.	Tax (Fed, State, FICA)		575
	NET SPENDABLE INCOME		1,515

Monthly Living Expenses

3.   Housing

Mortgage (Rent)	500	(rent)
Insurance		
Taxes		
Electricity	24	
Gas		
Water		
Sanitation		
Telephone	22	
Maintenance		
Assoc. Dues		
Other		
Total Housing		546

4.   Food — 125

5.   Automobile

Payments	350	('03 model)
Gas/Oil	20	
Insurance	100	
License/Taxes	15	
Maint/Repair	45	
Replace		
Total Automobile		530

6.   Insurance

Life	0	(Pd by company)
Medical	0	(Pd by company)
Other		
Total Insurance		0

7.   Debts

Credit Cards		
Loans/Notes	55	
Other		
Total Debts		55

8.   Entertainment & Recreation

Eating Out	450	
Baby Sitters		
Activities/Trips		
Vacation		
Other	35	(videos)
Total Entertainment & Recreation		485

9.   Clothing — 5

10. Savings — 0

11. Medical Expenses

Doctor	10	
Dentist	10	
Prescriptions		
Other		
Total Medical Expenses		20

12. Miscellaneous

Cosmetics		
Beauty/Barber	25	
Laundry/Cleaning		
Allowances		
Pets		
Subscriptions	10	
Gifts	250	
Christmas Gifts	300	
Other		
Total Miscellaneous		585

13. Investments — 66

14. School/Child Care

Tuition		
Materials		
Transportation		
Day Care		
Total School/Child Care		0

TOTAL LIVING EXPENSES — 2,417

Income Versus Living Expenses

Net Spendable Income	1,515
Less	
Total Living Expenses	2,417
Surplus or Deficit	-902

Section 4. Monthly Budget

Forms and schedules included:
1. Monthly Budget form (blank)
2. Monthly Estimated Budget
3. Month's Transaction List by day
4. January 2005 Monthly totals

Introduction:

A single adult posts her spending as the month progresses. The listing shown is a chronological record of spending that she has entered onto the Monthly Budget worksheet each week to ensure that she does not overspend in any category. By subtotaling after the 15th, it is easy to evaluate the income and spending for the first half of the month. If spending is too high in a category, restraint is necessary for the balance of the month to keep the category within budget.

Purpose of Form:

The Monthly Budget compares actual spending with planned spending as the days, months, and years go by. By recording transactions regularly, accountability to the budget becomes fairly simple.

Using the Monthly Budget form enables us to see how much is still available to spend in any category at any given time. Keeping a small calculator with the form speeds the process. Use the form for all spending (cash, check, debit card, credit card, electronic transfer, and so on). This form is not used to balance a checking account or credit card statement since all the forms of payment are being merged into one place.

This single adult has determined to get out of debt. To do so, she has committed to no more borrowing. Transactions that would have been done on a credit or charge card in the past are now being done with a debit card. A debit card is like an electronic check that withdraws money from the checking account when the transaction occurs. The payment on the Visa card is from past debt that is being paid off a little at a time.

For cash transactions, she either writes them down in a spending journal or keeps the receipts until she can enter them in her Monthly Budget form.

Assignment:

Please Note: All forms in this section include numbers to use for correct completion of the assignments. DO NOT USE your own personal budget numbers. Use the sample numbers provided.

Step One: Using the Monthly Estimated Budget (schedule 2), enter the budget amounts onto the blank Monthly Budget form for each category on the line labeled "Budget Amt." Total the spending categories and compare the total to the Income amount; they should be the same.

Step Two: Using the Monthly Transaction List (schedule 3), enter the spending onto the Monthly Budget form. Subtotal the spending by category on the MTD Subtotal line. Also total each at the end of the month on the Month Total line. After totaling the spending by category, compare the totals to the budget and calculate the surplus or deficit for each category for the month.

Using the January 2005 Monthly totals (schedule 4), add the category-by-category totals for February to the totals for January to fill in the YTD Budget and the YTD Tot Actual amounts. Then, calculate the YTD Surplus/Deficit for each category.

Using the numbers above, calculate and complete the This Month, Previous YTD, and Year to Date boxes at the bottom of the Monthly Budget form.

Submission of Completed Assignment:
Follow instructions provided by the instructor.

1.   Blank Monthly Budget Form

MONTHLY BUDGET

NAME OF STUDENT _____

FEBRUARY 2005

Category>	Income	1. Tithe/Giv.	2. Taxes	3. Housing	4. Food	5. Auto.	6. Insur.
Budget Amt.>	$	$	$	$	$	$	$
Day of Month							
1							
2							
3							
4							
5							
6							
7							
8							
9							
10							
11							
12							
13							
14							
15							
MTD Subtotal							
16							
17							
18							
19							
20							
21							
22							
23							
24							
25							
26							
27							
28							
29							
30							
31							
Month Total	$	$	$	$	$	$	$
Surplus/Deficit	$	$	$	$	$	$	$
YTD Budget	$	$	$	$	$	$	$
YTD Tot. Actual	$	$	$	$	$	$	$
YTD Surpl./Def.	$	$	$	$	$	$	$

Budget Summary

This Month

Total Income $ _____
Minus Total Spending $ _____
Equals Surplus/Deficit $ _____

+

Previous YTD

Total Income $ _____
Minus Total Spending $ _____
Equals Surplus/Deficit $ _____

=

38

MONTHLY BUDGET
NAME OF STUDENT _____
FEBRUARY 2005

7. Debt	8. Ent./Rec.	9. Clothing	10. Savings	11. Medical	12. Misc.	13. Invest.	14. Sch./Ch.
$	$	$	$	$	$	$	$
$	$	$	$	$	$	$	$
$	$	$	$	$	$	$	$
$	$	$	$	$	$	$	$
$	$	$	$	$	$	$	$
$	$	$	$	$	$	$	$

Year to Date

Total Income	$	_____
Minus Total Spending	$	_____
Equals Surplus/Deficit	$	_____

39

2. Monthly Estimated Budget

FEMALE SINGLE ADULT
AS OF JANUARY 2005

Monthly Income

GROSS INCOME PER MONTH:

Salary	1,975	
Interest	25	
Dividends		
Other		
Total Gross Income Per Month		2,000

LESS:

1. **Tithe/Giving** — 230

2. **Tax (Fed, State, FICA)** — 415

   NET SPENDABLE INCOME — 1,355

Monthly Living Expenses

3. **Housing**

Mortgage (Rent)	463	(rent)
Insurance		
Taxes		
Electricity	19	
Gas		
Water		
Sanitation		
Telephone	25	
Maintenance		
Assoc. Dues		
Other		
Total Housing		507

4. **Food** — 103

5. **Automobile**

Payments	98	
Gas/Oil	23	
Insurance	95	
License/Taxes	10	
Maint/Repair	50	
Replace		
Total Automobile		276

6. **Insurance**

Life		
Medical	47	
Other		
Total Insurance		47

7. **Debts**

Credit Cards		
Loans/Notes	22	
Other		
Total Debts		22

8. **Entertainment & Recreation**

Eating Out	125	
Baby Sitters		
Activities/Trips		
Vacation		
Other	20	
Total Entertainment & Recreation		145

9. **Clothing** — 5

10. **Savings** — 15

11. **Medical Expenses**

Doctor	10	
Dentist	10	
Prescriptions		
Other		
Total Medical Expenses		20

12. **Miscellaneous**

Cosmetics		
Beauty/Barber	35	
Laundry/Cleaning		
Allowances		
Pets		
Subscriptions	5	
Gifts	100	
Christmas Gifts	75	
Other		
Total Miscellaneous		215

13. **Investments** — 0

14. **School/Child Care**

Tuition		
Materials		
Transportation		
Day Care		
Total School/Child Care		0

TOTAL LIVING EXPENSES — 1,355

Income Versus Living Expenses

Net Spendable Income	1,355
Less	
Total Living Expenses	1,355
Surplus or Deficit	0

3. Month's Transaction List by day

Date	Amnt Rcvd	Amnt Paid	Paid By	Paid To/From	Paid For
February 1, 2005		30.00	Cash	First Church	Monthly Missions Giving
February 1, 2005		12.53	Debit Card	Denny's	Lunch with church group
February 2, 2005	780.00		Paycheck	Employer	Salary Net of Withheld Taxes
February 2, 2005		98.75	Check #2034	First Church	Tithe on Gross Paycheck
February 2, 2005		462.55	Check #2035	Eden Apartments	Monthly Rent
February 2, 2005		10.55	Debit Card	Quik Gas	Gas in Car
February 3, 2005		33.45	Debit Card	Main Street Market	Groceries
February 6, 2005		9.75	Cash	McDonald's	Dinner after working late
February 6, 2005		14.50	Debit Card	Borders Books	Pasta Cookbook (on sale)
February 6, 2005		25.00	Debit Card	Starbucks	Gift Card for friend
February 7, 2005		12.75	Cash	Center Cinema	Movie, Hot Dog, Popcorn & Drink
February 9, 2005		78.35	Debit Card	Reliable Auto	Scheduled car service
February 10, 2005		15.25	Debit Card	Applebees	Dinner after work
February 10, 2005		22.00	Check #2036	Visa Card	Monthly budgeted payment
February 11, 2005		12.53	Debit Card	Greengrocer, Inc	Fresh Produce
February 12, 2005		10.00	Check #2037	Dr. Smith	Medical Visit Co-Pay
February 13, 2005		19.50	Check #2038	Consolidated Edison	Electric Bill
February 13, 2005		20.53	Debit Card	Texas Steakhouse	Dinner with Friends
February 16, 2005	780.00		Paycheck	Employer	Salary Net of Withheld Taxes
February 16, 2005		98.75	Check #2039	First Church	Tithe on Gross Paycheck
February 16, 2005		98.00	Auto Debit	Ocean Credit Union	Car Payment
February 16, 2005		15.00	Auto Debit	Ocean Credit Union	To Savings Account
February 16, 2005		23.75	Check #2040	AT&T	Phone Bill
February 17, 2005		47.00	Auto Debit	USA Medical	Medical Insurance Premium
February 18, 2005		29.97	Debit Card	Main Street Market	Groceries
February 18, 2005		15.75	Cash	Pizza Heaven	Delivered Pizza
February 18, 2005		4.13	Cash	Blockbuster Video	Movie Rental
February 19, 2005		25.75	Debit Card	Lakeview Gifts	Christmas Gift bought ahead
February 21, 2005		15.85	Debit Card	Target	Socks and other clothing
February 24, 2005		25.00	Cash	Collection at work	Boss's birthday
February 25, 2005		10.00	Auto Debit	Daily Tribune	Bi-monthly subscription payment
February 25, 2005		9.45	Debit Card	Quik Gas	Gas in Car
February 26, 2005		40.23	Debit Card	Main Street Market	Groceries
February 27, 2005		119.50	Check #2041	Motor Vehicle Dept	Annual Auto Registration
February 28, 2005		25.00	Cash	Hair Affair	Wash & Set
February 28, 2005	22.50		Auto Credit	Ocean Credit Union	Interest on Bank CD
February 28, 2005		2.25	Check #2042	First Church	Tithe on Interest Earned
February 28, 2005		18.52	Debit Card	Zorba's	Lunch with church group

4. January 2005 Monthly Totals

(for use in completing the February 2005 Monthly Budget form)

Income	$1,578.75
Tithe/Giving	$229.38
Taxes	Netted out of Income
Housing	$507.76
Food	$113.77
Auto	$171.00
Insurance	$47.00
Debt	$22.00
Ent/Rec	$106.57
Clothing	$0.00
Savings	$15.00
Medical	$20.00
Misc	$100.64
Investment	$0.00
Schl/Chld	$0.00

Page Left Blank Intentionally

Section 5. *Savings Account Allocation*

Forms and schedules included:

1. Savings Account Allocations form (blank)
2. Monthly Estimated Budget form
3. January 2005 Monthly Budget

Introduction:

A couple with no children have created a budget that includes a number of annual, semi-annual, and other non-monthly payments. Their auto insurance is paid every six months. Auto registration and life insurance are paid annually. Their vacation is during the summer, when their company has its annual shutdown for plant maintenance. They do not buy any Christmas gifts in January. They want to buy a new living room sofa after Christmas this year to take advantage of the after-Christmas sales.

To ensure that there are funds allocated for these periodic needs, the Savings Account Allocation form is used as money is moved into the savings account. By tracking money moved from checking into the Savings Account by category, the contents of the savings account are clearly identified when needs arise.

Purpose of Form:

The Savings Account Allocation form is the final piece of a complete budgetary control system. When excess money accumulates in a checking account, there is temptation to look at the balance in the checking account rather than the category balances. This often results in spending money intended for another purpose. By actually transferring the excess funds to a savings account, the checking account is kept at a working level and the money being saved for specific purposes or under-spent in various categories can be identified in the savings account for future needs.

It is important to remember that these are not just book entries. The total amount moved on the Savings Account Allocation form must be transferred either by electronic means or by writing a check. Having both accounts at the same bank simplifies this task.

Assignment:

Please Note: All forms in this section include numbers to use for correct completion of the assignments. DO NOT USE your own personal budget numbers. Use the sample numbers provided.

Using the Monthly Estimated Budget form and the January 2005 Monthly Budget, transfer excess money and the monthly savings allocation into the savings account. Using February 1 for a transaction date, make the proper entries into the Savings Account Allocations form to reflect moving surplus moneys listed above from the checking account into the savings account.

Excess money is defined for the exercise as any money above $50 in any category (except Savings) at the end of the month. All money in the Savings category should be entirely transferred each month leaving a zero balance. In addition, money should be moved back from the savings account to bring any account category that has been overspent up to a zero balance.

Submission of Completed Assignment:

Follow instructions provided by the instructor.

1. Savings Account Allocations Form

NAME OF STUDENT _____

2005

Savings Account Allocation							
Date	Deposit	Withdrawal	Balance	Housing	Food	Auto Insurance	Auto Maint.
1/1/2005	Bal. Fwd.	from '04	10,082.25	25.00		190.00	135.25

NAME OF STUDENT _____
2005

Savings Account Allocation							
Insurance	Clothing	Gifts	Auto Registr.	Sofa Fund	Vacation	Savings Emer. Fund	Degree Completion
375.00	125.00				582.00	8,500.00	150.00

Page Left Blank Intentionally

2. Monthly Estimated Budget

COUPLE WITH NO CHILDREN
AS OF JANUARY 2005

Monthly Income

GROSS INCOME PER MONTH:

Salary	4,450
Interest	35
Dividends	100
Other	
Total Gross Income Per Month	**4,585**

LESS:

1. **Tithe/Giving** — **525**

2. **Tax (Fed, State, FICA)** — **1,050**

    NET SPENDABLE INCOME — **3,010**

Monthly Living Expenses

3. **Housing**

Mortgage (Rent)	850
Insurance	
Taxes	
Electricity	25
Gas	10
Water	
Sanitation	
Telephone	30
Maintenance	
Assoc. Dues	
Other (sofa fund)	100
Total Housing	**1,015**

4. **Food** — **235**

5. **Automobile**

Payments	135
Gas/Oil	43
Insurance	95
License/Taxes	15
Maint/Repair	65
Replace	
Total Automobile	**353**

6. **Insurance**

Life	125
Medical	15
Other	
Total Insurance	**140**

7. **Debts**

Credit Cards	
Loans/Notes	73
Other	
Total Debts	**73**

8. **Entertainment & Recreation**

Eating Out	105
Baby Sitters	
Activities/Trips	
Vacation	97
Other	20
Total Entertainment & Recreation	**222**

9. **Clothing** — **75**

10. **Savings** — **200**

11. **Medical Expenses**

Doctor	25
Dentist	20
Prescriptions	15
Other	
Total Medical Expenses	**60**

12. **Miscellaneous**

Cosmetics	7
Beauty/Barber	35
Laundry/Cleaning	10
Allowances	
Pets	15
Subscriptions	5
Gifts	95
Christmas Gifts	85
Other	
Total Miscellaneous	**252**

13. **Investments** — **100**

14. **School/Child Care**

Tuition	250
Materials	35
Transportation	
Day Care	
Total School/Child Care	**285**

    TOTAL LIVING EXPENSES — **3,010**

Income Versus Living Expenses

Net Spendable Income	**3,010**
Less	
Total Living Expenses	**3,010**
Surplus or Deficit	**0**

3. January 2005 Monthly Budget

MONTHLY BUDGET
COUPLE WITH NO CHILDREN
JANUARY 2005

Category>	Income	1. Tithe/Giv.	2. Taxes	3. Housing	4. Food	5. Auto.	6. Insur.
Budget Amt.>	$ 3,535.00	$ 525.00	Net fr Pychk	$ 1,015.00	$ 235.00	$ 353.00	$ 140.00
Day of Month							
1							
2	1,700.00	255.00	Net fr Pychk	850.00			
3					100.00	10.50	
4							
5							
6							
7						135.00	
8							
9							
10				25.00		8.50	
11							
12				10.00			
13						59.00	
14							
15							
MTD Subtotal	1,700.00	225.00	0.00	885.00	100.00	213.00	0.00
16	1,700.00	225.00	Net fr Pychk				15.00
17					95.00	7.75	
18							
19							
20				28.75			
21							
22							
23		75.00					
24						8.25	
25					25.00		
26							
27							
28							
29							
30							
31	135.00					7.95	
Month Total	$ 3,535.00	$ 525.00	$ 0.00	$ 913.75	$ 220.00	$ 236.95	$ 15.00
Surplus/Deficit	$ 0.00	$ 0.00	Net fr Pychk	$ 101.25	$ 15.00	$ 116.05	$ 125.00
YTD Budget	$ 3,535.00	$ 525.00	$ 0.00	$ 1,015.75	$ 235.00	$ 353.00	$ 140.00
YTD Tot. Actual	$ 3,535.00	$ 525.00	$ 0.00	$ 913.75	$ 220.00	$ 236.95	$ 15.00
YTD Surpl./Def.	$ 0.00	$ 0.00	Net fr Pychk	$ 101.25	$ 15.00	$ 116.05	$ 125.00

Budget Summary

This Month		Previous YTD	
Total Income	$ 3,535.00	Total Income	$ 0.00
Minus Total Spending	$ 2,774.22	Minus Total Spending	$ 0.00
Equals Surplus/Deficit	$ 760.78	Equals Surplus/Deficit	$ 0.00

+   **=**

50

MONTHLY BUDGET
COUPLE WITH NO CHILDREN
FEBRUARY 2005

7. Debt	8. Ent./Rec.	9. Clothing	10. Savings	11. Medical	12. Misc.	13. Invest.	14. Sch./Ch.
$ 73.00	$ 222.00	$ 75.00	$ 200.00	$ 60.00	$ 252.00	$ 100.00	$ 285.00
	20.00					50.00	
	3.95				5.00		
				15.00			
				15.00			
					50.00		
					10.00		
	18.56	55.36					
	3.95				25.00		
					2.50		
0.00	46.46	55.36	0.00	30.00	92.50	50.00	0.00
	21.25					50.00	
	7.50						
							250.00
73.00							65.00
					45.00		
				10.00			
	13.50				10.00		
	3.95						
					5.00		
				15.00			
	12.50						
	7.50						
$ 73.00	$ 112.66	$ 55.36	$ 0.00	$ 55.00	$ 152.50	$ 100.00	$ 315.00
$ 0.00	$ 109.34	$ 19.64	$ 200.00	$ 5.00	$ 99.50	$ 0.00	$ (30.00)
$ 73.00	$ 222.00	$ 75.00	$ 200.00	$ 60.00	$ 252.00	$ 100.00	$ 285.00
$ 73.00	$ 112.66	$ 55.36	$ 0.00	$ 55.00	$ 152.50	$ 100.00	$ 315.00
$ 0.00	$ 109.34	$ 19.64	$ 200.00	$ 5.00	$ 99.50	$ 0.00	$ (30.00)

Year to Date

Total Income	$	3,535.00
Minus Total Spending	$	2,774.22
Equals Surplus/Deficit	$	760.78

Section 6. *Additional Schedules*

1.   **Understanding the Budget Categories**

GROSS INCOME PER MONTH: This category captures all income whether taxable or not, including items such as child support or inheritance money received. Estimate any irregular or lump-sum income; a prior year's tax return may help you estimate. Convert all numbers in this category to monthly amounts by taking the annual totals and dividing by 12. Make sure to enter gross monthly earnings before any payroll deductions.

CATEGORY 1 – TITHE / GIVING: This category captures all giving to the church and Christian ministries. Giving to other charitable organizations (Heart Fund, Boys and Girls Club, etc.) can be included here or under Category 12 – Miscellaneouss.

CATEGORY 2 – TAXES: Federal withholding, Social Security, state and local taxes should be included here. Self-employed individuals should use this category to set aside money for quarterly estimated tax payments. Beware of the tendency to treat unpaid tax money as windfall profit.

OTHER DEDUCTIONS: Deductions for insurance, credit union savings or debt payments, bonds, stock programs, retirement, and union dues should be included in gross income and deducted in their proper categories (Insurance, Savings, Debt, Investments, Miscellaneous). This provides a more comprehensive picture of where money is being spent and aligns more accurately with the guideline budget.

NET SPENDABLE INCOME (Gross Income less Tithe and Taxes) is the portion available for family spending. Please note that "Net Pay" on a pay stub is not the same as "Net Spendable Income."

CATEGORY 3 – HOUSING EXPENSES: This category includes all monthly expenses necessary to operate the home including rent or mortgage payments, taxes, insurance, maintenance, and utilities. The amount used for utility payments should be an average monthly amount, which can be obtained by calling the utility providing the service. If renting, be sure to secure renter's insurance. If you are unable to pinpoint the exact amounts you have spent for maintenance, use five percent of the monthly mortgage payment.

CATEGORY 4 – FOOD EXPENSES: This category is for all monthly grocery expenses including paper goods and nonfood products that you normally purchase at grocery stores. Make sure to include any similar items you buy at convenience stores or warehouse clubs. Do not include restaurants or fast food purchased and eaten away from home. Those expenses will be tracked separately in Category 8 – Entertainment/Recreation.

CATEGORY 5 – AUTOMOBILE EXPENSES: All monthly expenses of operating a car, including payments, insurance, gas, oil, maintenance, and money set aside to purchase the next car are included here. Total annual maintenance spending should be divided by

12 to estimate the monthly expense. The monthly portion of any annual or semiannual auto insurance payments should be set aside monthly to avoid a future cash crisis.

CATEGORY 6 – INSURANCE: This includes health, life, and disability insurances, but not those associated with the home, vacation homes, automobiles, or recreation vehicles.

CATEGORY 7 – DEBTS: This category does not include your home mortgage or automobile payments, but it does include all other monthly payments required to meet past debt obligations including payments to family or friends. Monthly payments for old credit card debt belong here. If you use a credit card for current expenses, however, those amounts should be captured in the appropriate category. Pay the total bill for those amounts when the bill comes—along with whatever monthly payment you make to reduce the old debt on that card. Better yet—pay current expenses with a check or debit card.

CATEGORY 8 – ENTERTAINMENT/RECREATION: Vacation savings, camping trips, sporting equipment, hobby expenses, and athletic events are included. Don't forget eating out, babysitting, and daily lunches purchased away from home. This category is easier to control by using cash instead of credit cards.

CATEGORY 9 – CLOTHING: Since clothing is frequently bought using credit cards, prior clothing costs are often buried in debt payments. Try to determine an annual amount and divide it by 12.

CATEGORY 10 – SAVINGS: Every family should allocate something for savings. Not only does a savings account provide funds for emergencies, it is a key element in good planning and financial freedom. Keep these funds in an easily accessible place such as a savings account or a money market account with check privileges and no penalties for early withdrawal. This category should not be confused with funds allocated for investing even though investing is sometimes referred to as "retirement savings," "college savings," and so on.

CATEGORY 11 – MEDICAL/DENTAL EXPENSES: This includes insurance deductibles, doctors' bills, eyeglasses, prescriptions, counseling fees, orthodontist visits, etc. Use a yearly average divided by 12 to determine a monthly amount. Health insurance premiums should be listed in Category 6 – Insurance.

CATEGORY 12 – MISCELLANEOUS: Include expenses that do not seem to fit anywhere else: pocket allowance (coffee money), miscellaneous gifts, Christmas presents, toiletries, and haircuts. Miscellaneous spending is usually underestimated. To get a clear picture of your spending habits in this category, you will need to monitor it carefully for at least two months. Self-discipline is the key to controlling miscellaneous spending. This category is another good candidate for using cash only. Create a list of specifics to be paid from this category in order to keep it from becoming the leak that never stops flowing.

CATEGORY 13 – INVESTMENTS: This category is for long-term investing, retirement, or college savings. Regular savings (building an emergency reserve) is captured in Category 10 – Savings. As debt-free status is achieved, more money can be diverted to this category.

CATEGORY 14 – SCHOOL/CHILD CARE: Use this category for expenses associated with children and school activities, including the cost of childcare. (Important Note: This is an *optional* category. The Percentage Guideline Schedules allocate 100% of income before considering this category. Any funds allocated to this category must be trimmed from other budget categories to keep the budget balanced. Make sure to reduce other categories to make up for any percentage of income that you allocate here.)

2. Percentage Guideline Schedules

Schedules Include:

a. Family of 2 (Married Couple with no Children)

b. Family of 4 (Married Couple with 2 Children)

c. Family of 4 – High Priced Housing Market (Married Couple with 2 Children)

d. Family of 6 (Married Couple with 4 Children)

e. Single Adult

f. Single Parent

a.   Family of 2 (Married Couple with no Children)

Percentage Guideline Schedule

Gross Income (Annual)	$15,000	$25,000	$35,000	$45,000	$55,000	$65,000
Gross Income (Monthly)	$1,250	$2,083	$2,917	$3,750	$4,583	$5,417
1. Tithe/Giving	10%	10%	10%	10%	10%	10%
2. Taxes[1]	8.8%	14.3%	18%	20.2%	21.5%	23.3%

Net Spendable percentages below add to 100%.						
3. Housing	38%	38%	34%	30%	27%	27%
4. Food	15%	12%	12%	12%	11%	10%
5. Auto	15%	15%	12%	12%	12%	11%
6. Insurance	5%	5%	5%	5%	5%	5%
7. Debts	5%	5%	5%	5%	5%	5%
8. Entertain./Recreation	4%	5%	6%	6%	7%	7%
9. Clothing	4%	5%	5%	5%	6%	6%
10. Savings	5%	5%	5%	5%	5%	5%
11. Medical/Dental	5%	5%	5%	4%	4%	4%
12. Miscellaneous	4%	5%	6%	7%	7%	8%
13. Investments[2]	-	-	5%	9%	11%	12%

[1] Guideline percentages for tax category include taxes for Social Security, federal, and a small estimated amount for state, based on 2002 rates.

[2] This category is used for long-term investments planning, such as college education or retirement.

b. Family of 4 (Married Couple with 2 Children)

Percentage Guideline Schedule

Gross Income (Annual)	$25,000	$35,000	$45,000	$55,000	$65,000	$85,000	$115,000
Gross Income (Monthly)	$2,083	$2,917	$3,750	$4,583	$5,417	$7,083	$9,583
1. Tithe/Giving	10%	10%	10%	10%	10%	10%	10%
2. Taxes[1]	*2.7%	11.2%	14.8%	17.2%	18.8%	23.5%	26.3%

Net Spendable percentages below add to 100%.							
3. Housing	39%	36%	32%	30%	30%	30%	29%
4. Food	15%	12%	13%	12%	11%	11%	11%
5. Auto	15%	12%	13%	14%	14%	13%	13%
6. Insurance	5%	5%	5%	5%	5%	5%	5%
7. Debts	5%	5%	5%	5%	5%	5%	5%
8. Entertain./Recreation	3%	5%	5%	7%	7%	7%	8%
9. Clothing	4%	5%	5%	6%	6%	7%	7%
10. Savings	5%	5%	5%	5%	5%	5%	5%
11. Medical/Dental	5%	6%	6%	5%	5%	5%	5%
12. Miscellaneous	4%	4%	6%	6%	7%	7%	7%
13. Investments[2]	-	5%	5%	5%	5%	5%	5%

If you have the expense below, the percentages shown must be deducted from the other budget categories							
14. School/Child Care[3]	8%	6%	5%	5%	5%	5%	5%

[1] Guideline percentages for tax category include taxes for Social Security, federal, and a small estimated amount for state, based on 2002 rates.

[2] This category is used for long-term investments planning, such as college education or retirement.

[3] This category is added as a guide only. If you have this expense, the percentage shown must be deducted from other budget categories.

* In some cases earned income credit will apply. It may be possible to increase the number of deductions to lessen the amount of tax paid per month. Review the last tax return for specific information.

c. Family of 4 – High Priced Housing Market (Married Couple with 2 Children)

Percentage Guideline Schedule

Gross Income (Annual)	$45,000	$55,000	$65,000	$85,000	$115,000
Gross Income (Monthly)	$3,750	$4,583	$5,417	$7,083	$9,583
1. Tithe/Giving	10%	10%	10%	10%	10%
2. Taxes[1]	14.8%	17.2%	18.8%	23.5%	26.3%

Net Spendable percentages below add to 100%.					
3. Housing	55%	50%	46%	45%	40%
4. Food	11%	11%	11%	11%	11%
5. Auto	11%	12%	12%	12%	13%
6. Insurance	4%	4%	4%	4%	4%
7. Debts	4%	4%	4%	4%	4%
8. Entertain./Recreation	3%	4%	5%	5%	5%
9. Clothing	2%	3%	4%	4%	5%
10. Savings	2%	2%	3%	3%	5%
11. Medical/Dental	5%	5%	5%	4%	4%
12. Miscellaneous	3%	4%	4%	4%	5%
13. Investments[2]	-	1%	2%	4%	4%

If you have the expense below, the percentages shown must be deducted from the other budget categories					
14. School/Child Care[3]	5%	5%	5%	5%	5%

[1] Guideline percentages for tax category include taxes for Social Security, federal, and a small estimated amount for state, based on 2002 rates.

[2] This category is used for long-term investments planning, such as college education or retirement.

[3] This category is added as a guide only. If you have this expense, the percentage shown must be deducted from other budget categories.

d. Family of 6 – (Married Couple with 4 Children)

Percentage Guideline Schedule

	$25,000	$35,000	$45,000	$55,000	$65,000
Gross Income (Annual)	$25,000	$35,000	$45,000	$55,000	$65,000
Gross Income (Monthly)	$2,083	$2,917	$3,750	$4,583	$5,417
1. Tithe/Giving	10%	10%	10%	10%	10%
2. Taxes[1]	*1.7%	9%	9.8%	12.8%	15.1%

Net Spendable percentages below add to 100%.					
3. Housing	38%	38%	34%	33%	32%
4. Food	15%	15%	14%	14%	14%
5. Auto	14%	14%	12%	12%	11%
6. Insurance	5%	5%	5%	5%	5%
7. Debts	5%	5%	5%	5%	5%
8. Entertain./Recreation	3%	4%	4%	5%	5%
9. Clothing	5%	5%	6%	6%	7%
10. Savings	4%	4%	5%	5%	5%
11. Medical/Dental	8%	7%	7%	7%	7%
12. Miscellaneous	3%	3%	5%	5%	5%
13. Investments[2]	-	-	3%	3%	4%

If you have the expense below, the percentages shown must be deducted from the other budget categories					
14. School/Child Care[3]	10%	8%	6%	6%	5%

[1] Guideline percentages for tax category include taxes for Social Security, federal, and a small estimated amount for state, based on 2002 rates.

[2] This category is used for long-term investments planning, such as college education or retirement.

[3] This category is added as a guide only. If you have this expense, the percentage shown must be deducted from other budget categories.

* In some cases earned income credit will apply. It may be possible to increase the number of deductions to lessen the amount of tax paid per month. Review the last tax return for specific information.

e.   **Single Adult**

Percentage Guideline Schedule

	Living Alone	With Roommate	Living Alone	With Roommate
Gross Income (Annual)	$23,000	$23,000	$32,000	$32,000
Gross Income (Monthly)	$1,916	$1,916	$2,667	$2,667
1. Tithe/Giving	10%	10%	10%	10%
2. Taxes	19.7%	21%	21.9%	24%

Net Spendable percentages below add to 100%.				
3. Housing	40%	25%	38%	22%
4. Food	6%	6%	6%	6%
5. Auto	15%	20%	15%	20%
6. Insurance	4%	4%	4%	4%
7. Debts	5%	5%	5%	5%
8. Entertain./Recreation	7%	9%	6%	9%
9. Clothing	5%	7%	5%	6%
10. Savings	5%	8%	5%	13%
11. Medical/Dental	6%	6%	4%	3%
12. Miscellaneous	5%	5%	7%	7%
13. Investments[1]	2%	5%	5%	5%

If you have the expense below, the percentages shown must be deducted from the other budget categories				
14. School[2]	3%	10%	7%	10%

[1] This category is used for long-term investments planning, such as college education or retirement.

[2] This category is added as a guide only. If you have this expense, the percentage shown must be deducted from other budget categories.

f.   Single Parent

Percentage Guideline Schedule

Gross Income (Annual)	$15,000	$20,000	$25,000
Gross Income (Monthly)	$1,250	$1,667	$2,083
1. Tithe/Giving	10%	10%	10%
2. Taxes[1]	3.2%	6.7%	11.8%

Net Spendable percentages below add to 100%.			
3. Housing	40%	39%	39%
4. Food[2]	15%	14%	14%
5. Auto	15%	14%	14%
6. Insurance	3%	3%	4%
7. Debts	4%	5%	5%
8. Entertain./Recreation	3%	4%	4%
9. Clothing	5%	5%	5%
10. Savings	5%	5%	5%
11. Medical/Dental	7%	7%	6%
12. Miscellaneous	3%	4%	4%
13. Investments[3]	-	-	-
14. School/Child Care[4]	-	-	-

[1] This percentage is based upon year 2002 rates for Social Security, federal, and state taxes. This does not factor the Earned Income Credit, which may alter this figure considerably.

[2] This percentage is for money spent on food and does not include the reduction that would result by food stamp or food bank use.

[3] Considering the obligations at this income level, there may be no surplus funds for investing long term.

[4] This category is added as a guide only. If you must pay for childcare, all other categories must be reduced to provide funds for this expense. Although this is a real need, many single parents have alternative arrangements to meet the need through family or scholarship programs.

[*] In some cases earned income credit will apply. It may be possible to increase the number of deductions to lessen the amount of tax paid per month. Review the last tax return for specific information.

Part IV. Additional Resources

Section 1. *House Pay-down*

This section offers suggestions on ways to reduce mortgage debt through making extra payments or using an alternate buying strategy. Extra house payment suggestions should not be implemented until all consumer debt has been paid off. An effective way to pay down consumer debt quickly is listed in Part IV, Section 2, Debt Pay-down.

House Pay-down:

There are two popular ways to shorten the length of a mortgage. The first is to add an extra amount to each month's payment; the second is to make one complete extra payment per year. These are contrasted below.

Mortgage Pre-Payment Comparison $300,000 borrowed at 6 percent				
	Typical Mortgage (No Extra Payments)	Extra Monthly Payment	Extra Monthly Payment	Extra Annual Payment
Extra Monthly Payments Made	$0	$100	$200	
Extra Annual Payment Made	$0			$1,799
Total to Pay to Term	$647,515	$594,178	$556,351	$576,600
Total Interest Saved	$0	$53,337	$91,164	$70,915
Months of Payments	360	313	279	297
Months Reduced	0	47	81	63
Length Loan Reduced by	0	3 years and 11 months	6 years and 9 months	5 years and 3 months

A common recommendation when making extra payments on a mortgage is to write a separate check for the extra payment and mark in the memo field to apply it to principal only. This helps the mortgage company apply the payment as it should. You might also want to calculate the effect your extra payment(s) should have each year and compare it to the year-end statement. You may have to request a year-end statement from the mortgage company.

This analysis assumes that extra payments will start soon after the loan is created. Interest savings will diminish if extra payments start later. Inconsistent extra payments will also diminish the savings shown above. The general principle of saving interest expense by paying more than the required minimum can be applied to almost any kind of debt.

Biggers / Smalls Analysis:

When dealing with a purchase rather than an existing loan, the analysis of the Biggers and Smalls reveals another way to move more quickly toward financial freedom. The question is whether to buy your dream house as soon as possible, or buy something less expensive and move into the dream house later.

This analysis involves two couples, the Biggers and the Smalls. The Biggers are the typical homebuyers who get the biggest house they can afford right away. The Smalls are disciplined home buyers who decide they can live in a smaller home for a few years to save a significant sum of money. Both couples have $60,000 to spend as a down payment. They both desire to own a house that costs $300,000.

Biggers / Smalls

The Biggers go ahead and buy their $300,000 house with a 6 percent, 30-year mortgage. Their monthly payment is $1,439 and at the end of their mortgage they will have paid a total of $578,012 for the house.

The Smalls decide that they can live in a smaller home for a while in a less expensive neighborhood. They buy a house for $180,000 with a 5 percent, 7-year mortgage. Their monthly payment is $1,696 and at the end of this mortgage, they will have paid a total of $202,470 for this house.

Note that the Smalls get a lower interest rate on their mortgage because the term is shorter. The shorter term will require extra discipline in their budget to pay the extra $257 per month versus the Biggers, but the Smalls have a goal and are working toward it. A longer-term mortgage will have a higher interest rate, but it can still be treated like a seven-year loan by making large enough payments each month—as illustrated in the House Pay-down example. There is also some additional safety with a longer-term mortgage in the event of lean times, since the extra principal payments each month would be optional rather than required.

At the end of the first 7 years, the Biggers are still making payments on their 30-year mortgage.

At the end of the first 7 years, the Smalls sell their newly debt-free house and buy the house next door to the Biggers. They apply the total value of the old house ($180,000) as a down payment on their new one ($300,000). Once again, they do a 7-year loan at 5 percent and their payments are still $1,696.

We understand that interest rates and house prices change during a span of seven years. However, they could change in favor of the Smalls. In addition, the savings illustrated here are so large that the changes in house prices and interest rates are likely to be insignificant compared to the savings.

At the end of the 14 years, the Biggers are still making payments on their 30-year mortgage. In fact, they are just now making reasonable principal payments. The 169th payment (the first payment in the 15th year of their loan) is comprised of $552 of principal and $887 of interest).

The Smalls now have a debt-free home which cost them $344,940 overall. However, the good news doesn't stop there. They are so used to making payments of $1,696, that they start making those payments into an investment earning 4 percent. When the Biggers pay off their house (16 years later), the Smalls have over $455,000 in the bank.

Overall, both families have the debt-free home of their dreams, but the Smalls got there sooner and have a significant amount of money in the bank from their efforts.

Section 2. *Debt Pay-down*

Once the decision has been made to get out of debt, there is an easy technique for speeding the process. Modifications can always be made, but keep in mind that they usually weaken the benefit by postponing the final debt payment.

We'll begin with an example and then give instructions.

EXAMPLE: The Smith Family
The Smith family completed their List of Debts form using the following steps:

1. They looked back into their financial history to ensure that they listed every outstanding debt. Had they not taken that step, they might have overlooked the personal loan from Uncle Joseph.

2. They listed the debts in the order of the balance due, highest at the top to lowest at the bottom. Even though the mortgage and the car loan are not part of the debt category on the other forms, they do belong on this form.

3. They totaled the columns containing the monthly payments and the balances due.

4. They made three important commitments within the family:

    • They will always pay the $2,348 monthly total of debt payments until every debt is eliminated.

    • They are praying for God to help them eliminate their debt.

    • They will incur no new debt. To accomplish that, they have budgeted savings each month to make future purchases (including replacement of cars).

5. They started working their plan on January 1, 2004. Their form is illustrated below.

LIST OF DEBTS
SMITH FAMILY
AS OF JANUARY 1, 2004

Creditor/Item Purchased	Monthly Payment	Balance Due	Payment Date (Day of Mo.)	Scheduled Payoff Date	Interest Rate	Past Due Amount
E Scrooge, Mortgage	$1,530.00	$191,560.00	10	12/10/2032	8.75%	None
Auto Finance Corp, Loan	$321.00	$11,689.00	15	9/15/2008	11.5%	None
National School Loan	$200.00	$7,794.00	3	5/3/2009	14.5%	None
NBank MasterCard	$118.00	$5,381.00	17	6/17/2007	18.5%	None
Super Bank Visa	$109.00	$4,949.00	10	4/10/2007	19.8%	None
Uncle Joe (Repair Trans.)	$50.00	$1,250.00	15	1/15/2007	0%	None
Mervyn's Credit	$10.00	$449.00	1	11/1/2004	19.8%	None
Sears Credit	$10.00	$140.00	1	6/19/2004	24%	None
Totals	$2,348.00	$223,212.00				

In mid-January, a late Christmas gift arrives from an aunt who lives quite a distance away. Since she did not want to ship things, she sent a check for $200. A typical family would probably spend the money on a trip or something for the home. However, the Smiths have made a commitment, and they regard this as an answer to their prayer for God's help. So after tithing on the gift, they use $140 of it to pay off the Sears Credit debt. The balance is used for other things.

Many families would then consider the $10 per month reduction in their debt obligation as a windfall and figure out another place to spend it. But the Smiths have committed not to pay any less than $2,348 per month until every debt is eliminated. So, they add the $10 per month from the Sears Credit debt to the Mervyn's Credit payment (the next one up on the list), bringing it to $20 per month starting in February.

At the same time, they will mark off the Sears Credit debt from the List of Debts and close the account (if they haven't already done so). The modified list is shown below.

LIST OF DEBTS
SMITH FAMILY
AS OF JANUARY 1, 2004

Creditor/Item Purchased	Monthly Payment	Balance Due	Payment Date (Day of Mo.)	Scheduled Payoff Date	Interest Rate	Past Due Amount
E Scrooge, Mortgage	$1,530.00	$191,560.00	10	12/10/2032	8.75%	None
Auto Finance Corp, Loan	$321.00	$11,689.00	15	9/15/2008	11.5%	None
National School Loan	$200.00	$7,794.00	3	5/3/2009	14.5%	None
NBank MasterCard	$118.00	$5,381.00	17	6/17/2007	18.5%	None
Super Bank Visa	$109.00	$4,949.00	10	4/10/2007	19.8%	None
Uncle Joe (Repair Trans.)	$50.00	$1,250.00	15	1/15/2007	0%	None
Mervyn's Credit	$20.00	$449.00	1	11/1/2004	19.8%	None
~~Sears Credit~~	~~$10.00~~	~~$140.00~~	~~1~~	~~6/19/2004~~	~~24%~~	~~None~~
Totals	$2,348.00	$223,072.00				

Later in the spring, there is an opportunity for one of the family members to work a weekend inventory at a local company. The net after tithe and taxes from the job is enough to pay off the reduced Mervyn's Credit debt. Once again, the Smiths remember their commitment and regard this as an answer to their prayers. They pay off the Mervyns Credit debt and add the $20 per month from the Mervyn's Credit debt to the payment to Uncle Joseph, bringing it to $70 per month. They also mark off the Mervyns Credit debt and close the account. The modified list of debts is shown below.

This raises a common question: Would it be better to pay off the loan with the lowest balance first or the loan with the highest interest? That depends on which motivates you more:

- quickly eliminating a debt entirely so that you can apply its payment to the next debt, or

- saving more interest by reducing a larger debt that has very high interest even though it will take longer to eliminate that debt.

Sometimes paying a little extra interest is worth the reinforcement that comes from completing a solid step toward a long-term goal. And those steps come more quickly by paying the smallest balances first.

LIST OF DEBTS
SMITH FAMILY
AS OF JANUARY 1, 2004

Creditor/Item Purchased	Monthly Payment	Balance Due	Payment Date (Day of Mo.)	Scheduled Payoff Date	Interest Rate	Past Due Amount
E Scrooge, Mortgage	$1,530.00	$191,560.00	10	12/10/2032	8.75%	None
Auto Finance Corp, Loan	$321.00	$11,689.00	15	9/15/2008	11.5%	None
National School Loan	$200.00	$7,794.00	3	5/3/2009	14.5%	None
NBank MasterCard	$118.00	$5,381.00	17	6/17/2007	18.5%	None
Super Bank Visa	$109.00	$4,949.00	10	4/10/2007	19.8%	None
Uncle Joe (Repair Trans.)	$70.00	$1,250.00	15	1/15/2007	0%	None
~~Mervyn's Credit~~	~~$20.00~~	~~$449.00~~	~~1~~	~~11/1/2004~~	~~19.8%~~	~~None~~
~~Sears Credit~~	~~$10.00~~	~~$140.00~~	~~1~~	~~6/19/2004~~	~~24%~~	~~None~~
Totals	$2,348.00	$223,623.00				

The process then continues in the same manner until all of the debt is paid off including the car and the house. Since the Smiths are following God's principles, he has blessed them in unexpected ways and is prospering their plans. *"Commit to the LORD whatever you do, and your plans will succeed"* (Proverbs 16:3).

Self-implementation:

To implement this process in your own finances, complete your own List of Debts as illustrated in this section. Begin with the highest payoff amount and end with the lowest. Once again, it is important to list the minimum payments for credit cards and other revolving loans. When all the debts are listed, total the "Monthly Payment" and "Balance Due" columns.

At this point, make the same three commitments the Smiths made.

1. Always pay at least the current monthly total of debt payments until every debt is eliminated (this was $2,348.00 for the Smiths—even after retiring some debts so that their contractually required payments were lower).

2. Ask God to help you eliminate your debt. Handling money is a spiritual issue.

3. Incur no new debt. Stop borrowing and begin saving. Both are necessary for a debt-free existence as well as the process of getting there.

With those commitments in place, start making the payments and watch the plan work. When we work toward financial freedom so that we can serve God more effectively, He blesses our efforts. We get out of debt more quickly and we learn to trust Him more fully. Both are components of financial freedom.

Warning: You will reach a point in this process where the only debt left is the family home mortgage. The temptation is to stop making extra payments because you don't want to lose a tax deduction. But until the tax rate exceeds 100%, a tax deduction is not a good reason to have a debt. Consider this:
* Assume that John is in a 30 percent tax bracket and pays $1,000 in tax-deductible mortgage interest.

* John gets a tax savings of $300.

* John nets a $700 cash loss.

Suppose John decides to pay off the mortgage and lose his deduction:
* John does not pay $1,000 because the mortgage has been paid off.

* Because he has lost the tax deduction, John has to pay $300 more in taxes.

* John nets a $700 gain to save or spend.

Some people, however, really want to limit their tax payments because of political, moral, or emotional, reasons. For them it can look like this:
* John pays off his mortgage but wants to reduce his payment of taxes. He makes a $1,000 donation to his church or favorite ministry.

* Because of his 30 percent tax bracket, John gets a tax savings of $300.

The church or ministry nets a $1,000 gain, and John saves $300 in taxes—a double benefit!

Section 3. *On-Line Tools*

A growing number of tools exist to help you create and maintain a working budget. We have listed just some of them here.

As of completion of this manuscript, all of the sites listed were available to the public and did not collect personal information for the use of the tools. You should, however, always exercise caution in revealing identifiable personal information when using online resources.

We make no claim that the free tools or the materials offered for sale on these sites will fit your specific needs.

- www.crown.org – Click on "tools." Calculators provided include an Online Budget Guide, a Budgetometer, a How Much Do You Really Make Calculator, a Credit Card Minimum Payment Calculator, a Lease/Purchase Calculator, a Mortgage Prepayment Calculator, a 15 vs. 30 Year Calculator, and a Personality ID Test.

- www.daveramsey.com – tools to calculate mortgages, investing, and other financial subjects. Also contains a "quickie" budget program.

- http://www.thinkglink.com/financial-calculators.asp – calculators for loans, refinancing, amortization, loan buy down, buying versus renting, debt consolidation, mortgage qualifying, and closing costs.

- http://www.aba.com/Consumer+Connection/CNC_pfin.htm – calculators for affordable mortgages, auto payments, college savings, mortgage payments, mortgage refinancing, and renting or buying.

- http://www.usatoday.com/money/perfi/calculators/calculator.htm – calculators for home mortgages, retirement, credit cards, automobiles, personal loans, home equity loans, IRAs, budgeting, savings, insurance, mutual funds, stocks, and bonds.

- http://cgi.money.cnn.com/tools – calculators for debt, budgeting, mutual fund screening, college savings plans, insurance, mortgages, retirement, spending, savings, and currency conversion.

- www.studentloanconsolidator.com – a calculator to project payments on refinanced student loans. Also has good information to help one understand the student loan process and rules.

Section 4. *Book, Software, and Web Resources*

Many financial education resources can enhance your further study. We have chosen some of the more influential books of the last decades to include in this list. Most of them are available either through online booksellers or local Christian bookstores.

Books:

- *Business by the Book* by Larry Burkett, published by Thomas Nelson Publishers, Nashville, TN

- *The Challenge of the Disciplined Life* by Richard J. Foster, published by HarperSanFrancisco, San Francisco, CA

- *The Christian's Guide to Effective Personal Management* by Kenneth W. Oosting, published by JKO Publishing, Franklin, TN

- *Debt-Free Living* by Larry Burkett, published by Moody Publishers, Chicago, IL

- *Financial Parenting* by Larry Burkett and Rick Osborne, published by Moody Publishers, Chicago, IL

- *Financial Peace: Revisited* by Dave Ramsey, published by Penguin Putnam Inc., NY, NY

- *Getting Your Financial House in Order* by David and Debbie Bragonier, published by Broadman and Holman Publishers, Nashville, TN

- *Generous Living* by Ron Blue, published by Zondervan Corp., Grand Rapids, MI

- *God and Your Stuff* by Wesley K. Wilmer, published by NavPress, Colorado Springs, CO

- *It's Your Money, Isn't It?* by G. Edward Reid, published by Review and Herald Publishing, Hagerstown, MD

- *New Master Your Money* by Ron Blue, published by Moody Publishers, Chicago, IL

- *Money, Possessions and Eternity* by Randy Alcorn, published by Tyndale House Publishers, Wheaton, IL

- *Neither Poverty nor Riches* by Craig L. Blomberg, published by Intervarsity Press, Downers Grove, IL

- *Rich Christians in an Age of Hunger* by Ronald J. Sider, Published by Word Publishing, Dallas, TX

- *Smart Money* by Jerry & Ramona Tuma and Tim LaHaye. published by Multnomah Publishers, Sisters, OR

- *Splitting Heirs* by Ron Blue, published by Northfield Publishing, Chicago, IL

- *Sound Mind Investing Handbook* by Austin Pryor, published by Sound Mind Investing, Louisville, KY

- *Total Money Makeover* by Dave Ramsey, published by Thomas Nelson Publishers, Nashville, TN

- *Treasure Principle* by Randy Alcorn, published by Multnomah Publishers, Sisters, OR

- *Using Your Money Wisely* by Larry Burkett, published by Moody Publishers, Chicago, IL

- *Wealth to Last* by Larry Burkett and Ron Blue, published by Broadman and Holman Publishers, Nashville, TN
- *The Word on Finances* by Larry Burkett, published by Moody Publishers, Chicago, IL
- *The World's Easiest Guide to Finances* by Larry Burkett, published by Northfield Publishing, Chicago, IL
- *Your Money Counts* by Howard Dayton, published by Crown Financial Ministries, Gainesville, GA

Workbooks:
- *The Crown Small Group Biblical Financial Study* by Howard Dayton, published by Crown Financial Ministries, Gainesville, GA
- *The Crown Collegiate Small Group Bible Study* by Howard Dayton, published by Crown Financial Ministries, Gainesville, GA
- *Every Single Cent* by Larry Burkett with Brenda Armstrong, published by Crown Financial Ministries, Gainesville, GA
- *Faith & Money: A Practical Theology of Wealth* by Howard Dayton and Chad Cunningham, published by Crown Financial Ministries, Gainesville, GA
- *The Family Financial Workbook* by Larry Burkett, published by Moody Publishers, Chicago, IL
- *The Financial Guide for the Single Parent* by Larry Burkett with Cheri Fuller, published by Moody Publishers, Chicago, IL
- *How To Manage Your Money* workbook by Larry Burkett, published by Moody Publishers, Chicago, IL

Software:
- Budgeting Program – *Money Matters 2005*, published by Crown Financial Ministries, Gainesville, GA
- Credit Rating Management – *Credit Check*, published by Crown Financial Ministries, Gainesville, GA
- Donation Valuation and Tracking – *It's Deductible*, published by Intuit, Mountain View, CA
- Financial Calculators – *Snapshot Gold*, published by Crown Financial Ministries, Gainesville, GA

Websites:
- Crown Financial Ministries – www.Crown.org
- Generous Giving – www.GenerousGiving.org
- Good Sense Ministry – www.goodsenseministry.com
- Eternal Perspectives Ministry – www.epm.org
- Vision Resourcing – www.visionresourcing.com
- Christian Financial Professionals Network – www.cfpn.org

Section 5. *Scriptural Resources*

BORROWING
Exodus 22:14; Deuteronomy 15:1-11; Psalm 37:25; Proverbs 3:27-28, 22:7; Matthew 5:25-26, 5:40, 18:23-35; Luke 12:58-59

CHILDREN
Psalm 127:3; Proverbs 1:8, 6:20, 10:1, 13:1, 15:5, 15:20, 17:25, 19:18, 22:6, 23:13, 23:22, 29:15, 29:17; Ephesians 6:4

CONTENTMENT
Psalm 119:14, 119:57, 119:72; Proverbs 3:13, 8:18-21, 10:22; Matthew 20:1-16; Philippians 4:11-14; Colossians 3:2; 1 Thessalonians 5:18; 1 Timothy 3:3, 6:6-9; 1 John 2:15

COSIGNING
Proverbs 6:1, 11:15, 17:18, 19:19, 20:16, 22:26-27

COUNSEL
Proverbs 12:5, 12:15, 13:20, 14:7, 14:15, 15:22, 19:20, 24:6, 27:9

DISHONESTY
Exodus 22:9, 23:8; Leviticus 6:1-2; Deuteronomy 27:17-19; Psalm 15:5, 37:37, 62:10, 119:113; Proverbs 2:15, 10:10, 11:1, 11:18, 11:20, 13:25, 15:27, 16:30, 17:8, 17:23, 20:10, 20:14, 22:28, 23:10, 24:8; Jeremiah 9:4; Luke 16:1-9

EGO
Psalm 75:4, 107:40; Proverbs 11:2, 12:9, 15:25, 16:18-19, 18:12, 18:23, 19:1, 28:11, 28:25, 29:23, 30:7-8; Jeremiah 9:23, 22:21; Matthew 19:27, 23:12; Luke 14:11; Philippians 2:3; 1 Timothy 6:17; James 5:1-5

ENVY
Psalm 73:2-3; Proverbs 23:17, 24:19; Matthew 20:1-16

EXCELLENCE
Proverbs 18:9, 22:29; Colossians 3:17; 1 Peter 4:11

GREED
Proverbs 21:17, 22:16, 23:6-7; Ecclesiastes 2:10, 4:8, 5:10, 5:13; Jeremiah 8:10; Amos 5:11; Matthew 6:19, 6:24, 19:23, 23:14, 25:45; Luke 12:13-15, 12:16-20, 16:14, 16:19-21; Acts 5:1-10; Ephesians 5:5; 1 Timothy 6:10; 2 Timothy 3:2; Titus 1:11; Hebrews 13:5; James 3:14-16, 4:3

HONESTY
Deuteronomy 25:14-15; Psalm 112:1-3; Proverbs 10:3, 10:9, 13:5, 13:21, 15:6, 16:11, 20:7, 22:1, 22:4, 24:16, 28:6, 28:18; Luke 16:10-14, 19:8

INHERITANCE
Proverbs 20:21; Ecclesiastes 2:21, 6:3

INVESTING
Psalm 62:10, 127:2; Proverbs 11:28, 17:12, 21:5, 23:4-5, 28:20-22; Matthew 25:14-30; Luke 19:12-26

LAZINESS
Proverbs 12:27, 13:4, 14:4, 19:15, 19:24, 20:4, 21:25, 22:13, 24:30, 26:13

LENDING
Exodus 22:25-26; Deuteronomy 23:19-20, 24:10; Nehemiah 5:7, 5:10; Psalm 15:5, 37:26; Proverbs 28:8; Ezekiel 18:8; Luke 6:34-35, 7:41

PLANNING
Proverbs 16:1, 16:3, 16:8, 19:21, 20:5, 28:18, 24:3, 24:27, 27:1, 27:12, 27:23; Luke 14:28-30; Ephesians 4:14

SAVING
Proverbs 6:6-10, 21:20; Psalm 37:25; Matthew 6:19-20

SHARING

Exodus 16:18-20; Psalm 72; Proverbs 11:24, 14:21,21:13, 22:9, 28:27; Matthew 5:42, 6:3, 10:42, 13:12, 24:45, 25:40; Mark 12:41-44; Luke 6:38, 10:35; Acts 2:45, 4:32; Romans 10:15, 12:13; 1 Corinthians 9:7-11, 9:14, 16:1-2; 2 Corinthians 8:8-15, 9:6-13; Galatians 6:6; 1 Timothy 5:3, 5:8; 2 Timothy 2:4-6; James 2:15-16; 1 John 3:17; 3 John 6-7

SUING

Luke 6:30-36; 1 Corinthians 6:1-7

TAXES

Matthew 17:24-25; Mark 12:14; Luke 20:22-25; Romans 13:6-7

TITHE

Genesis 14:20; Exodus 25:1, 30:14-15, 34:19; Leviticus 27:30-34; Deuteronomy 12:6, 12:17, 14:22-29, 18:1-4, 26:12; 2 Kings 12:16; 2 Chronicles 31:4-6, 31:12; Nehemiah 10:32, 10:35-39, 13:12; Proverbs 3:9; Isaiah 66:20; Malachi 3:8-10; Matthew 5:23, 23:23; Luke 11:42; Hebrews 7:1-10

TRUST

Psalm 37; Jeremiah 17:7-8; Matthew 10:9, 16:24, 19:21; Mark 4:24, 6:9, 8:34; Luke 9:59-60, 10:4, 11:13, 14:33, 18:29, 22:35-36; Philippians 4:19

WIVES

Proverbs 12:4, 31:10-16; 1 Corinthians 11:3

WORK

Deuteronomy 24:14-15; Proverbs 6:6-10, 10:4-5, 12:11, 12:24, 14:23, 16:26, 28:19; Ephesians 4:28

WORRY

Psalm 50:14-15; Proverbs 12:25; Matthew 6:27-34; Philippians 4:6; 1 John 4:18

Section 6. *Blank Forms*

This section contains forms for creating and managing your own budget. Instructions for using each form can be found in its corresponding section in Part III of this workbook.

    a.   Monthly Estimated Budget form

    b.   List of Debts form

    c.   Budget Analysis form

    d.   Monthly Budget form

    e.   Savings Account Allocation form

    f.   Checkbook Ledger

MONTHLY ESTIMATED BUDGET
AS OF _____

Monthly Income

GROSS INCOME PER MONTH:

Salary _____
Interest _____
Dividends _____
Other _____
Total Gross Income Per Month ☐

LESS:

1. **Tithe/Giving** ☐

2. **Tax (Fed, State, FICA)** ☐

   NET SPENDABLE INCOME ☐

Monthly Living Expenses

3. **Housing**
   Mortgage (Rent) _____
   Insurance _____
   Taxes _____
   Electricity _____
   Gas _____
   Water _____
   Sanitation _____
   Telephone _____
   Maintenance _____
   Assoc. Dues _____
   Other _____
   Total Housing ☐

4. **Food** ☐

5. **Automobile**
   Payments _____
   Gas/Oil _____
   Insurance _____
   License/Taxes _____
   Maint/Repair _____
   Replace _____
   Total Automobile ☐

6. **Insurance**
   Life _____
   Medical _____
   Other _____
   Total Insurance ☐

7. **Debts**
   Credit Cards _____
   Loans/Notes _____
   Other _____
   Total Debts ☐

8. **Entertainment & Recreation**
   Eating Out _____
   Baby Sitters _____
   Activities/Trips _____
   Vacation _____
   Other _____
   Total Entertainment & Recreation ☐

9. **Clothing** ☐

10. **Savings** ☐

11. **Medical Expenses**
    Doctor _____
    Dentist _____
    Prescriptions _____
    Other _____
    Total Medical Expenses ☐

12. **Miscellaneous**
    Cosmetics _____
    Beauty/Barber _____
    Laundry/Cleaning _____
    Allowances _____
    Pets _____
    Subscriptions _____
    Gifts _____
    Christmas Gifts _____
    Other _____
    Total Miscellaneous ☐

13. **Investments** ☐

14. **School/Child Care**
    Tuition _____
    Materials _____
    Transportation _____
    Day Care _____
    Total School/Child Care ☐

    TOTAL LIVING EXPENSES ☐

Income Versus Living Expenses

Net Spendable Income ☐
    Less

Total Living Expenses ☐

Surplus or Deficit ☐

LIST OF DEBTS
AS OF _____

Creditor/Item Purchased	Monthly Payment	Balance Due	Payment Date (Day of Mo.)	Scheduled Payoff Date	Interest Rate	Past Due Amount
Total						

BUDGET ANALYSIS
AS OF _____

Income per Year: _____
Income per Month   _____

Monthly Payment Category	Existing Budget	Guideline Budget	Difference + or −	New Monthly Budget
1. Tithe/Giving				
2. Tax				
Net Spendable Income				
3. Housing				
4. Food				
5. Automobile				
6. Insurance				
7. Debts				
8. Entertain & Recreation				
9. Clothing				
10. Savings				
11. Medical				
12. Miscellaneous				
13. Investments				
14. School/Child Care				
Total Living Expenses (Total of 3-14)				
Difference				

MONTHLY BUDGET
MONTH OF _____

Category>	Income	1. Tithe/Giv.	2. Taxes	3. Housing	4. Food	5. Auto.	6. Insur.
Budget Amt.>	$	$	$	$	$	$	$
Day of Month							
1							
2							
3							
4							
5							
6							
7							
8							
9							
10							
11							
12							
13							
14							
15							
MTD Subtotal							
16							
17							
18							
19							
20							
21							
22							
23							
24							
25							
26							
27							
28							
29							
30							
31							
Month Total	$	$	$	$	$	$	$
Surplus/Deficit	$	$	$	$	$	$	$
YTD Budget	$	$	$	$	$	$	$
YTD Tot. Actual	$	$	$	$	$	$	$
YTD Surpl./Def.	$	$	$	$	$	$	$

Budget Summary

This Month
Total Income $ _____
Minus Total Spending $ _____
Equals Surplus/Deficit $ _____

+

Previous YTD
Total Income $ _____
Minus Total Spending $ _____
Equals Surplus/Deficit $ _____

=

MONTHLY BUDGET
MONTH OF _____

7. Debt	8. Ent./Rec.	9. Clothing	10. Savings	11. Medical	12. Misc.	13. Invest.	14. Sch./Ch.
$	$	$	$	$	$	$	$
$	$	$	$	$	$	$	$
$	$	$	$	$	$	$	$
$	$	$	$	$	$	$	$
$	$	$	$	$	$	$	$
$	$	$	$	$	$	$	$

Year to Date

Total Income	$ _____
Minus Total Spending	$ _____
Equals Surplus/Deficit	$ _____

SAVINGS ACCOUNT ALLOCATION FORM
STARTING ON _____

Savings Account Allocation							
Date	Deposit	Withdrawal	Balance	Housing	Food	Auto Insurance	Auto Maint.

SAVINGS ACCOUNT ALLOCATION FORM
STARTING ON _____

Savings Account Allocation							
Insurance	Clothing	Medical	Debts				

CHECKBOOK LEDGER
PAGE _____

Date	Check #	Transaction		Deposit	Withdrawal	Balance

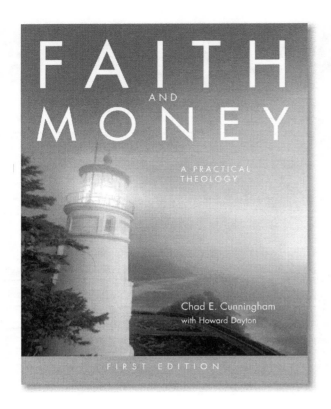

Faith and Money—A Practical Theology

Item Number: FM1010
ISBN: 978-1-56427-178-5

Faith and Money—
A Practical Theology

Most current college students possess a minimum of four credit cards and hold a balance on those cards of over $3,000. Additionally, most graduating college students will enter the work force carrying an average debt baggage of nearly $18,900 in student loans.

The need for the next generation of students to have academically appropriate and student-friendly materials that focus on the connection between faith and money is clear. **_Faith and Money—A Practical Theology_** textbook/curriculum fills that gap through theologically sound, integrative, and balanced teaching.

Features
- Appendices containing multiple charts and visual guides
- Practical Application
- Study Guides with Summary Questions
- Supplemental Reading List

For information on the Faith and Money _course, visit Crown.org or call 1-800-722-1976._
For inquiries in Canada, please contact CrownCanada.ca or call 1-866-401-0626.